Explaining Canada

A Primer For Yanks

Ken Stange

BOOKS BY

KEN STANGE

A Smoother Pebble, A Prettier Shell (Penumbra Press)
Advice To Travellers (Penumbra Press)
Bourgeois Pleasures (Quarry Press)
Bushed (York Publishing)
Cold Pigging Poetics (York Publishing)
Colonization Of a Cold Planet (Two Cultures Press)
Embracing The Moon (Two Cultures Press)
God When He's Drunk (Two Cultures Press)
Going Home (Two Cultures Press)
Love Is A Grave (Nebula Press)
More Than Ample (Two Cultures Press)
Nocturnal Rhythms (Penumbra Press)
The Sad Science Of Love (Two Cultures Press)
These Proses A Problem Or Two (Two Cultures Press)

Explaining Canada

A Primer for Yanks

~~

Ken Stange

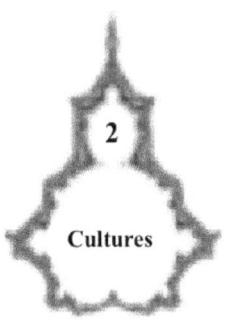

Two Cultures Press

2014

Copyright © 2008, 2014 by Ken Stange

All rights reserved.

For information about permission to reprint, record, or perform sections of this book, write to **Two Cultures Press**, 970 Copeland, North Bay, Ontario, Canada, P1B 3E4 (**info@twoculturespress.com**)

Library and Archives Canada Cataloguing in Publication

Stange, Ken, 1946-, author
    Explaining Canada : a primer for Yanks / Ken Stange.

ISBN 978-0-9809273-9-9 (pbk.)

    1. Canada--Social life and customs--Humor. 2. National characteristics, Canadian--Humor. 3. United States--Social life and customs--Humor. I. Title.

FC173.S726 2014   971.07'300207   C2014-903410-5

Acknowledgement

As always, I am infinitely indebted to my indefatigable editor, Ursula Stange. Without her, I would've been continuously embarrassing myself in print from the very start.

Cover Design: Ken Stange.
The artwork is based on a William Ludwig sculpture in New Orleans.

ISBN: 978-0-9809273-9-9

For Ursula, wife (fellow immigrant and former "alien" in the U.S. of A.), and my two home-grown (grown-up) Canuck 'kids', Christiaan and Katherine.

CONTENTS

FOREWORD — 7

INTRODUCTION AND DUBIOUS CREDENTIALS — 8

- DRINKING AND DINING — 12
- BEER: THE REAL STORY — 13
- BARS AND BOOZE: DRINKING UNDER DURESS — 19
- CUISINE: THE AWFUL ALMOST UNPALATABLE TRUTH — 27
- DINING OUT: A SURVIVAL GUIDE — 33

SEX, DRUGS AND ROCK 'N ROLL — 39

- SEX: BEATS THREE DOGS IN THE TENT TO KEEP WARM — 40
- HOMOSEXUALITY: QUEER VIEWS ON 'QUEERS' — 46
- THE STRAIGHT DOPE: OXYMORON FOR A CANUCK DRUGGIE — 48
- ROCK 'N ROLL OUT THE CARPET: IT'S LEGAL IN CANADA — 52

PALISADE PARK POLITICS — 54

- POLITICS: OUR QUIRKY SYSTEM — 55
- COMMIES: WHY CANUCKS ARE SUCH PINKOS — 60
- TERRORISTS: WHY CANUCKS ARE NOT PARANOID — 62
- ANTI-AMERICANISM: WHY CANUCKS DON'T LOVE THEIR NEIGHBOURS — 65

ARTSY AND ENTERTAINING—WELL SOMETIMES — 68

- CULTURAL PROTECTIONISM: NO UNGUARDED BORDERS FOR CULTURE — 70
- LITERATURE: CANUCKS CAN READ—AND REALLY DO — 73
- MUSIC: WE GAVE YA OUR BEST — 76
- FILM: IT AIN'T HOLLYWOOD BUT IT AIN'T BERGMAN EITHER — 79
- PERFORMING ARTS: SCALPING TICKETS AT THE RESERVE — 82

CANADA'S (SPLIT) PERSONALITY — 85

- TWO CULTURES: ACTUALLY THREE PLUS N — 86
- MORES AND FOLKWAYS: DEFERENCE DIFFERENCES — 89
- HUMOUR: OVER YOUR HEAD AND BELOW THE BELT — 92

REGIONAL DIFFS AND RIFFS — 99

- THE FAR NORTH — 101
- BC: BIG COAST WANNABES — 103
- THE PRAIRIE CHICKENS — 107
- ONTARIO: KING RATS IN A DIRTY NEST — 110
- QUEBEC: BIG POND FROGS — 113
- DOWN EAST: COD FISHERS AND COD PIECES — 117

FINAL WORDS—OF APOLOGY — 121

FOREWORD

I wrote this book eight years ago, more to get some things off my chest than to 'educate' Americans about their northern neighbours. So when it didn't immediately find a publisher, I was drawn into other writing projects. It ended up just being filed, where it just slept in a folder on my computer.

.

Recently, in the course of cleaning up a backlog of projects that I'd put on hold, I reread it. Canada has changed drastically since I wrote it, but I was pleasantly surprised to see the book wasn't hopelessly dated and that much of it still applied.

.

Of course, much really has changed. And, unfortunately, I can't say for the better. Canada has become more American in the worse possible ways. And the U.S. has become more like Canada in some good ways, although it has also become even more American in its more unfortunate characteristics.

.

I felt that if I appended an update to each section, the book still had worth. And I'm sure that my contrarian, opinionated attitude has remained unchanged enough to keep the tone of the book consistent. Yanks and Canucks should still both be annoyed by it.

—May 2014

INTRODUCTION AND DUBIOUS CREDENTIALS

"If the national mental illness of the United States is megalomania, that of Canada is paranoid schizophrenia." —Margaret Atwood

. Bartlett Brebner remarked that "Americans are benevolently ignorant about Canada, while Canadians are malevolently well informed about the United States." This book is a modest attempt to decrease that Yankee ignorance, albeit somewhat malevolently.

The first question—and it is a most reasonable one—to ask of someone with the chutzpah to claim to "explain" a country as vast and diverse and lunatic as Canada is: What qualifications does this presumptuous fellow possess? And a second question that any *American* reader who makes it through even a few of the following essays will undoubtedly ask is: "Where the hell does he get off mocking The Land Of The Free And Home Of The Brave?" And since I'm expecting some fellow Canadian citizens to read this as well, I'm sure they'll be asking: "Who the hell does this bloody immigrant think he is to make fun of our way of life?"

So I'll admit the title is pretty presumptuous. Of course I can't really *explain* Canada. It is as inexplicable as American pride in their nasty form of callous pseudo-democracy. I'm no political analyst or sociologist—and very glad not to be—and so all I really mean to imply by the title is that Yanks might find some of my remarks about my adopted homeland's idiosyncrasies insightful, just as my fellow citizens may find them reasonable cause to revoke my citizenship.

So let me say right off that I feel I have a *familial* right to say rude things about both Canucks and Yanks, for the situation is analogous to criticizing one's parents: most of us do it but oh boy do we get very, very annoyed if someone else does. Well, I spent the first two decades of my life in the allegedly 'United' States and the next three (and change) in Canada—with frequent forays back to the land of my birth. I am a legal citizen of both countries although Canada is now my true home. I think of America as Fatherland and Canada as Motherland. Thus I feel I have a right to comment on both Yank ignorance *and* Canuck inanity—because in both cases I am 'family.' You can't say it, but I can: *my father is a nut cake and my mother is a flake.*

One acquires a very special understanding of a place if one grows up there, an understanding that can never be matched by any Johnny-Come-Lately. It is analogous to language acquisition. If we try to learn a second language after puberty, we will always have an accent. We may *seem* to master the language, even write it at a virtuoso level (as Nabokov and Conrad obviously did), but it will always be a *second* language, and the careful listener will always be able to detect the accent, the odd turn of phrase. On the other hand, one gains a broader understanding of a place when one is away from it. (How many writers in 'exile' have defined their homeland in their works?) Absence may or may not make the heart grow fonder, but distance definitely does give one *perspective*.

This is my justification for having the gall to say what some will surely consider offensive things about both the alleged "Land Of The Free" *and* my adopted nation. My justification for claiming to be qualified to offer less than gracious explanations of the numerous quirks and idiocies of the country that welcomed me to its—albeit somewhat chilly (literally and figuratively)—bosom has to do with that aforementioned perspective gained from distance. The immigrant, unless sequestered in a ghetto, pays a lot of attention to local customs as part of his acculturation. And the absurdities of most of these customs, mores, and folkways are only obvious to someone new to them. Hell, the ethnocentric natives take them for granted. I remember my father-in-law (an immigrant from Germany) shaking his head at the North American reversal of common sense regarding drinking and having one's hair cut. Why, he asked, do Chicagoans insist that one engage in the social and friendly activity of having a few drinks only in dark, window-less, and often dungeon-like rooms called 'bars' (where sometimes there are, in fact, bars on the windows, places where children and dogs are forbidden entrance); but on the other hand, the private grooming activity of having one's hair cut is often done in a plate glass window where passers-by can gawk at the spectacle of your locks being shorn?

For Canadians, "defining" themselves (almost always in a compare-and-contrast essay featuring their southern neighbour) competes with hockey for the title of "National Pastime". Nonetheless, native born Canucks (those who had Canada thrust upon them by the happenstance of their parents' conjugal pleasures) really haven't a clue about how truly distinctive (read *weird*) they are. It takes an immigrant, an outsider, to see the absurdity of what seems natural to the native. So I hope the following compare-and-contrast essays by someone not particularly biased by experience limited to just one of the national units may be a bit more objective than most cultural commentaries on the great nations of Amerika and Kanada.

As a footnote to this résumé for the position for Cultural Critic and Canuck Explicator, I should add that I have repeatedly blundered about most of the countries of Europe and have some, albeit limited, experience of how more civilized people live. Although I wouldn't presume to explain why most Bulgarian women have their hair coloured in some—often otherworldly—shade of red or why allegedly grownup, and notoriously prim and proper Brits (and a people arguably on average far more literate than any other on our planet) use absurd diminutives for perfectly reasonable words (taking their dogs for "walkies" or rising in the morning to eat "brekie"), I have observed enough more rational behaviour in non-North American places to feel it gives me some larger context in which to place both Yank and Canuck idiosyncrasies.

I hope my observations don't so severely offend my fellow Canadians as to have me drummed out of my adopted land, for I'm sure my American readers then would promptly mount a campaign to keep me from spending my exile on the Yankee soil from which I once happily tore up roots. What would I do then? I'd have to go live in the Czech Republic or some *civilized* country—but where I couldn't speak the language and my LLD (Language Learning Disability) would restrict my social life to expat bars where homesick Yanks and Canucks would probably not be an entirely receptive audience to my Canuck (and Yank) bashing tirades. I'd probably end my days in some *pension* drinking beer (albeit *real* beer) alone in my room—and with someone taking way too long in the bathroom down the hall.

And, no, England would *not* be an option—for two reasons. First, contrary to the popular misconception, they do not speak my native tongue. Second, I said a *civilized* country. (What civilized nation closes their drinking establishments at eleven o'clock?)

But I guess there is Australia. But that would mean I'd be trapped on a desert island. What would I take to read? Germaine Greer? That's a scary thought! Oh the Aussies are another twisted story entirely.

Whatever. I offer these observations with no malice—or, well, maybe only a wee bit of malice. I offer them up specifically to Yanks, those southern neighbours of mine who are notoriously ignorant of Canucks (and just about everybody else). My fellow citizens may not particularly like my explication of their culture, but you can't please all of the people…etc. Besides, annoying people is far more fun than pleasing them.

Oh and that applies to using very politically incorrect nicknames for folks of varying ethnic origins, sexual proclivities, and even those with mental or physical problems. I think it is about time we realized that sticks and stones may break our bones, but words will never hurt us—at least not mortally. Anybody who thinks my using what is now considered 'offensive' terms means that I'm a bigot is a bloody idiot. (Excuse me—is a person mentally challenged.) But, hey, hate mail is welcome. And I have faith that neither of my countries are so vindictive as to revoke my citizenships on the basis of political incorrectness.

Drinking and Dining

I decided to put this section first because we're all animals, no matter our nationality, and the three basic animal needs—amply rewarded in our hyperactive little hypothalamuses for satisfying them—are eating, drinking, and getting laid. Eat, drink and have Mary—or Mark. I decided to deal with sex after eating and drinking because sex is always better if you have to wait for it. (Take him or her out for dinner first and then make your move.) And I decided to deal with beer first, because it probably is the one thing that both Yanks and Canucks would probably rank first as a cultural difference.

Beer: The Real Story

Yank Question: Someone said making love in a canoe is like American beer. What did they mean?

Canuck Answer: That they are both fucking close to water!

That is, of course, a Canadian joke. We are inordinately proud of the fact that our beer is allegedly stronger. And more *beer-like* than that damn Yankee piss. This isn't entirely true, but the myth is so wide-spread that even Americans buy into it. I've overheard tourists from Ohio in a local Northern Ontario watering hole carry on about how strong this Canuck beer is—largely, I think, to justify their obnoxious behaviour. Alcohol is, after all, a universal excuse for inappropriate behaviour.

So here is the head's up for Yanks. Most Canadian beer is 5% alcohol content. The so-called "Ice" beers are a bit stronger—as they are in The States. And we do, of course, have some very strong beers such as some of those brewed in Quebec. We don't however, unlike our southern neighbours, label our stronger beers "malt *liquor*"—as if that pushed them up there with the hard stuff. But, to my embarrassment, the average Canuck drinks one of the popular and tasteless swills such as Molson Canadian or Labatt Blue—which are 5% yet taste like water. Back south of the border the average beer drinker (the great majority, it seems) drinks Bud—which tastes like watered down water. But note the taste is deceiving: Bud is also 5%. So much for the myth! Yes, once many Yankee brews were 3.2%, but those days are past—except for some of the so-called 'light' beers.

It should be remembered that taste and alcohol content are not significantly correlated. The tastiest brews such as real pilsners and British ales and bitters are usually 4 point something percent, while most of the so-called strong 'ice' beers brewed in both Canada and the States have as about as much taste as ice. But then taste seems to be viewed as an undesirable characteristic of beer by both Yanks and Canucks, who consistently favour the flavourless—and then further dull what little taste the beverage might have by damn near freezing the poor thing before drinking it.

So: your Bud drinker comes north in the spring to catch some pickerel (or walleye as these Buddies call them) and, after the only bites he gets are blackfly bites, hits the local pub and swills some swill like Labatt's Blue with his new found Canuck buddy next to him at the bar—and then starts acting like a goof after only a few brew. Well, I think that has to be a nasty placebo effect—or innate Yankee social inappropriateness exacerbated by being away from home.

Let's talk about beer and beer appreciation and beer drinking behaviour in these two North American countries, as contrasted with a few other places. Beer culture is high culture and at the same time *volk* culture. Neo-barbarian freshmen at any university in the putatively civilized world quaff the stuff with only one intention: drunkenness. Then on the other hand there are snooty organizations (e.g., Prague's Club of Beer Connoisseurs), comparable to the wine connoisseur sub-culture, that are devoted to separating the watery swills from the flavourful pils. I don't think they taste a fine pilsner or ale or lager and then fastidiously spit it out and cleanse their palate with Evian water, but they are certainly more concerned with taste evaluation than with getting pissed out of their mind and doing a panty raid on the girls' dorm.

The Sumerians invented beer and even had a goddess of beer: Ninkasi. There are reputable scholars that maintain that the movement from hunter/gatherer society to an agrarian society was because of the need to hang around while the stale bread fermented into beer. Makes sense to me: I can buy that. There are few, if any, cultures where there is not some fermented (as opposed to distilled) drink that could be considered, given a loose enough definition, a form of beer. (E.g., sake is not a Japanese wine; it is a rice beer.)

Our current conception of what beer *is* has been shaped (although very distorted in North America) by the Germanic tradition of brewing. My *very* German mother-in-law, who attributes all significant intellectual, scientific and artistic accomplishments to Germans, is (annoyingly) correct in claiming that what most people in the world now call 'beer' is largely Germanic in origin. Yes, that Tsingtao you order at a Chinese restaurant is the result of a German colony in China that set up a brewery. But forget German chauvinism, many non-Germanic countries now make excellent beers—including, amazingly, the U. S. of A.

The States actually have more microbreweries cooking up good stuff than Canada, and many of them are excellent, producing exceptional brews that are widely distributed, so we Canucks shouldn't prance around like superior beer connoisseurs. Oh yes, Canada does have some excellent microbreweries, but the puritanical provincial liquor laws and the shipping costs over vast distances mean that most Canadians (unless they live in a major city) may actually have less choice when it comes to selecting a beer than the average Yank. But whether this is true or not, the fact remains that most Yanks don't know their aspen from a pole in the ground when it comes to beer. And they certainly don't give a rat's ass about taste. But should they, well then Canada has much to offer—if they look carefully.

·

So how to advise a Yank about beer in Canada? Well, there are two fundamental things a visitor from The South should know. One: you can't buy beer anywhere, anytime; the liquor laws in most of Canada are draconian, puritanical, and, in a word—*ridiculous*. Two: Canucks have a weird superiority complex about their beer, even when they drink horse piss, and this is true even when that horse piss is actually a Yank import that they're too drunk or ignorant to notice its origin.

·

To deal with the first, first. I live in Ontario, so I'll describe the situation here since I know it best, but most of Canada isn't very different. (Quebec is the exception: there you can buy beer—and wine—most reasonable hours at any "dep" or *dépanneur*—which is basically a convenience store.) We Ontarians have so-called "Beer Stores". We also have so-called "Liquor Stores". (You can get some brands of beer, especially the better imported beers not available at the Beer Stores, at the Liquor Stores, but you can't get liquor at the Beer Stores, except for a few 'girlie drinks'; i.e., premixed cocktails in beer bottles. Got that? Confusing? I know.) These Beer Stores are only open certain hours and certain days.

·

Many a thirsty visitor from south of the border has been stunned, shocked, and appalled to find he can't pick up a six pack for his bedtime snack or Sunday brunch. Most beer stores do not open until 10 a.m. and lock up tight no later than 10 p.m. Furthermore, until recently beer stores were closed on Sunday—although now they deign to open for 3 or 4 hours on Sunday afternoon, presumably after everyone is safely home from church and ready for a little of the hair of the dog that bit them Saturday night. And on certain National Holidays, when one would think it is most reasonable to relax with a brew, they have their lights out and doors secured. What about those Liquor Stores? Sorry. These generally keep the same hours—or occasionally are even more likely to have a large CLOSED sign posted when you most desire some suds.

·

Well at least there must be a lot of these 'beer stores' around, even if they keep limited hours, since Canucks are notorious beer consumers. Right? Wrong! I live in a community of 55 thousand people. We only have *three* beer stores and two of them close early. Yes, we do sometimes have lines at closing time—especially before a Holiday lockdown—but going to one of these beer stores usually isn't like queuing up for hours at the market in Soviet-era Moscow. Often one is the only customer. The Beery Canuck Myth needs some addressing.

This brings me to another notable point: the Canuck's superiority complex about beer—both consumption and appreciation. How misguided! At least Americans don't have pretensions about their beer. (Of course, being pretentious in America is a cardinal sin. Yanks like to pretend they are all 'just folks', and heaven help those who claim otherwise!) Except for the microbreweries and their largely Yuppie clientele, for most Yanks beer is "just beer". "Gimme a Bud." "Sure, buddy, Have five and see if you can pick up the waitress with your somewhat slurred witty remark about her cute transmission case." We Canadians, on the other hand, seem to consider it part of our national identity to be Beer People. "Beer ain't just for breakfast!" is our national motto. Stories at the local pub of drinking with Yanks almost always involve an episode where the poor southerner goes under the table early in the evening, because he just can't handle our sturdy suds, nor has he the training that young'uns up here get in 'holding' their liquor—well, not liquor actually, but beer. (Of course in Russia and large portions of Europe, beer is considered virtually equivalent to a soft drink.)

Unfortunately the reality is a bit disillusioning. The hard fact is that Yanks actually drink more beer per capita than Canucks. Neither, however, are even in the running re beer consumption when places like Ireland or England or Germany or The Czech Republic are in the competition. (The Czech Republic, beer consumption capital of the world, is a true beer-lovers paradise where the per capita annual consumption is 161 litres, and a pint at a 'local' costs a Canuck Buck. Virtually all Czechs—men, women *and* children—drink beer in this wonderful country, drink beer all the time—and, it should be noted, where drunks are far, far rarer than in either The States or Canada.)

Now of course the definition of 'beer' in these statistical analyses is extremely broad, for it includes such homeopathic concoctions as Coors Light. I say 'homeopathic' because the pseudo-science of homeopathy claims that if you dilute a poison sufficiently it cures the symptoms the poison produces. Well Coors tastes like water, but does contain some small amount of ethanol and if consumed in copious quantities can induce inebriation. So it follows by perverse homeopathic reasoning: water down the watery Coors and you can cure drunkenness! Never mind that cup of strong coffee before you aim your car home. Have a Coors Light.

.

But I digress. Here are the facts. Most Yanks and most Canucks drink an inferior beer-like product because they are stupid enough to be influenced by moronic beer commercials that suggest to adolescents that slugging back their Brand X brew will get them laid. The inferior beer-like products most Yanks drink are even more inferior and flavourless than the beer-like products Canucks drink, so even a Molsen Canadian may taste exotic. But then Canucks are prone to emulate the worse traits of their southern neighbours, so these inferior indistinguishable Yank beers (especially Bud and Coors and Millers; collectively called "Budmillors") are actually becoming more and more popular up here—where we really should know better.

.

So, yes Canadians do like to drink beer and do so a lot, but in fact less so than Yanks. Our typical popular swill is definitely superior to the typical Yank swill, but this is hardly reason for us to feel superior and sophisticated. (Go to Europe, you naïf!) In short, on average we actually drink slightly less beer but a slightly better beer. And residents of both countries are really country bumpkins who should travel more—especially to Europe where real beer is appreciated.

.

To return to advising mode: Yanks who travel to Canada and think Bud is beer will find it here and should just be careful to stock up whenever our Big Brother Government permits one to purchase anything with alcohol in it. Yanks who do really appreciate beer with taste *can* find a wonderful variety of quality beers if they just avoid the big brewery products (E.g., Labatts and Molson).

.

One final note. Canadians tend to buy their beer in cases of 24 and so any Yank hoping to 'pass' should walk up to the counter at The Beer Store and speak in the local idiom: "Gimme a *two-four* a Canadian." A cumbersome case of 24 Molsen Canadian will come flying out on the roller ramp from the bowels of the store. The bottles will be in the inconvenient and bulky long-necked format that replaced the traditional, sensible 'stubbies' we used to have before we adopted (yet only another too-typical emulation of our southern neighbours) this odd way of bottling brew.

.

Oh well. It *is* common ground, this beer thing Yanks and Canucks have. Maybe a little more 'common' in every sense of the word than we Canadians would like to admit, but hey good neighbourly relations are often cemented over a pint.

Update

There is little that needs updating here. Both the States and Canada have more microbreweries. And in both countries there are more people who appreciate beer that has some taste, but the majority still are content with their Buds and Molson's.

Bars and Booze: Drinking Under Duress

Yank Question: How come it is that while most major cities in the good ol' U.S. of A. have a bar on every other corner, most major Canadian cities have, instead, a bank?

Canuck Answer: Yanks like to drink. Canucks like to bank.

Well that isn't the whole explanation. Drinking in public is a complicated issue in Canada and requires some explication. And I can't really explain why we have so many banks—which actually are all branches of a handful of staid national banks, unlike The States where so-called "Savings and Loans" and other fly-by-night financial institutions blight the landscape. But I can give a—perhaps biased—historical and cultural explanation of why most places in Canada unfortunately do not have the 'locals' so common in Europe and The States.

The first thing I need to point out is that there are major regional differences, although not nearly as great as in The States, but the most important distinction is between Quebec and the rest of the country, which is to say between what was originally French Canada and what was originally English Canada. Quebec is a special case, and the local bar is as much a part of their culture as it is in most European nations. But the Quebecois, as they never cease to remind the rest of the country, are a "distinct society". So let me deal with them separately.

What we now call English Canada was once British Canada, and one could argue that it was originally populated by the most conservative of the Brits that came over The Pond, the Loyalists. For whatever reason our southern neighbours got the misfits and rebels, those less than loyal to the British Monarchy. So The United States was formed by violent revolution and Canada was formed by—well I'm not sure what the right word is, perhaps apathy. Whatever, we just hung around until we were eventually granted independence. I am sure this simplistic description would give any historian an apoplectic fit, but my point, regarding public imbibing in Canada, is simply that our Anglophone founding fathers were a pretty sober lot and brought with them the worst of British stuffiness, which became incorporated in our laws.

19

But that's ancient history. Let me present more recent history; i.e., my own first-hand experiences when I first came to this fair land. Things have changed since 1968, but old inhibitions regarding imbibition die hard.

My friend Neil and I arrived in Toronto early in 1968 to scout the place out. We were typically ignorant Yanks whose knowledge of Canada was limited to its general location somewhere up above Chicago and its apparent willingness to harbour draft dodgers. My graduation was approaching and with it the virtual certainty that if I tried to stay home I would end up far from it—sent into a distant jungle, assigned to snuffing gooks and trying not to get snuffed myself. (Being an outspoken agnostic, I couldn't claim conscientious objector status which was only granted to members of select religious cults.) Five years in jail held little appeal, and that left just Sweden and Canada. I am not good with languages and so Sweden was a distant second. So I really already had decided on Canada.

To my naïve, uninformed mind it was just a gentler, kinder version of my fatherland. It seemed that Canadians didn't believe in waging war against peasants in some far away jungle for no apparent reason, and furthermore they harboured young men holding the same beliefs. They spoke American, and yet they spoke out against Americans. Their popular Prime Minister, this Trudeau guy, wore sandals and was rumoured to be an intellectual and a leftist and a ladies man. And they had great film theatres and book stores and universities and concerts and radio stations and hippy communes and radical students. All this sounded utopian and too good to be true. Still, I had to check it out, do a reconnaissance mission before my wife and I packed up our meagre belongings the day after my final final exam to head North. (Canada also had, I'd heard, mail service, so I could skip graduation and have my diploma mailed to me.)

Cadre, the war resistors' organization that greased the rails of the underground railway, had as its two major stations: Toronto and Vancouver. Being in Chicago, Toronto was my logical destination.

First impressions were all very positive. Even today, Yanks are impressed with the cleanliness of Toronto compared to whatever messy, dirty city they hale from. (I find this amazing, living as I do in a community of 55,000 which by comparison makes Toronto look like a dumpster.) But being "spic and span" is the Canadian image, and it certainly was my initial impression of the place. (The only other thing that struck me as strongly, back in 1968, was how many attractive women promenaded on these pristine streets.)

After wandering Toronto's main drag, Yonge Street, gawking in awe at this vibrant downtown, my friend Neil and I decided we'd stop for a beer. (The author at last returns from his digression!) And it was then we noticed the plethora of banks and scarcity of bars. We realized we hadn't seen a single sign saying "Bar". I, however, eventually spotted a sign that said "Tavern". Minor difference in dialect, I immediately assumed. We, thirsty travellers, homed in on it.

"Fran's" it was called, and the chain still exists. We entered the establishment, which didn't look like any bar or tavern I'd ever been in. In fact it looked exactly like what in our fatherland is called a "family restaurant". We sat ourselves down in a booth and opened the menu. There was typical 'family restaurant' fare listed, burgers and all the usual stuff, but there was also a list of beers available. This struck me as bizarre, for in my fatherland so-called 'family' restaurants didn't serve anything alcoholic. (If you bring the family, then Mom and Dad presumably wouldn't even think of having a glass of beer with their meal, for that wouldn't be in accord with 'family values'.) So, I thought to myself, they call it a tavern for inexplicable reasons, but it ain't really: it's a 'family restaurant' that, being in a more liberal country, also serves drinks.

The waitress came over to take our order.

"I'll just have a beer," I said.

"You have to eat something," she replied.

"Huh? You concerned with my health?" I answered back, amazed at the level of caring in this country.

"You can't drink without having something to eat."

This level of caring was a bit too paternalistic, I felt.

I ordered some fries which I left untouched as I quaffed my beer and wondered if I might just be overestimating Canada's liberalism.

Well, after we moved up to Toronto, I learned the ins and outs of the arcane and archaic laws that 'regulated' public consumption of anything alcoholic. I can't speak with authority about the rest of the country, although friends and acquaintances assure me it wasn't very different elsewhere, and one of the times I was in Vancouver many years later, and not that many years ago, I remember having to order a plate of cookies with my beer so I could sit at an outdoor patio and people watch. (The waitress confided in me that the same plate of cookies had been doing the rounds a very long time, and I probably didn't really want to try any of them.)

Anyway, let me report the situation in 1968 in Toronto, for although things have definitely changed, enough remains the same as to be instructive for any thirsty Yank in Canada now. I'll describe how it was then and then how it now is: now as a result of then.

Then you could get a beer in "Toronto The Good" (as it was referred to in those days) at three types of places: 1) a 'tavern'; 2) a 'public house' or 'pub'; and 3) a 'hotel'.

A *tavern* was a term for a restaurant licensed to serve alcoholic beverages. The license came with strings attached: you had to eat something with the booze. In every place I'd been to in The States, 'tavern' meant 'bar'—a dark and dingy—albeit often friendly—place to drink. And it was a place where, if it did sell food, you wouldn't want to eat the stuff—at least not until you'd had too much to drink to go out in search of a real restaurant. In Canada it meant (and still largely means) an ordinary, or even fine, restaurant "licensed" to serve alcoholic drinks with the meals it serves. Things have finally changed and I believe most taverns across our vast land will now allow you just to have a drink—or even several, should you cho0se to eschew the food offerings. But, generally speaking, Yanks visiting Canada still shouldn't equate 'tavern' with 'bar'.

Now, on the other hand, a *pub* or 'public house' was a specific place devoted to drinking, but just beer! Yes, just beer—draft beer. Again things have changed, but a bit of historical background is still instructive to those who want to understand Canadian attitudes toward public consumption of alcoholic beverages. Shortly after my arrival in Toronto, I began exploring the 'pub scene'. This scene did not match up well with the beer commercials one sees on the tube, for it wasn't a music video with lithesome lassies flirting with young macho males. These pubs were barn-like structures where beat-up looking working-class guys sat at little round tables and quaffed many little glasses of draft beer until it was time to go home to the Missus. As in England until very recently, many of these places closed at 11 p.m. sharp.

One of the most famous of these pubs (and it is still around and still famous, although the rules and clientele have drastically changed) was the Brunswick House, near downtown Toronto, on Brunswick Avenue, just off Bloor Street. I'd become involved in an amateur (to put it mildly and kindly) theatre production that was to be staged at a place called The Poor Alex, which happened to be across the street from the Brunswick House. After a dress rehearsal one evening right before opening night, many of those involved with the production decided to celebrate the fact that most people remembered most of their lines by having a few at The Brunswick.

Now pubs in those days were segregated. There were two separate areas with separate entrances: one, the main one, was for "Men Only"; the other one was labelled "Ladies And Escorts". One can only speculate, but presumably proper ladies (as opposed to improper ladies of the night) only could enter a drinking establishment if properly 'escorted' by a man. So single—or wannabe single—men in the Men's Section couldn't hope for any loose women to come and join them at their little round tables filled with little glasses of draft. The other section, presumably, was a concession to the Missus who might want to join her hubbie for a pint. Single guys still could drink there, but most seemed to prefer the Men's section, since although the Ladies And Escorts section did allow women, all those women were 'escorted' and so accounted for.

Well, frankly, in those days at least, the Men's room *was* a men's room in terms of ambience—while the Ladies and Escorts room had some slight semblance of class. Anyway, a few women in the theatrical cast were willing to join us, to venture into this notorious pub, but, alas, we all were stopped at the door—because it seemed there was also some legal ratio of ladies to their escorts. Nine guys, or whatever we totalled up to, could not act as escorts to a mere three ladies. (These gals weren't 'ladies' by any stretch of the imagination, but that is another story.) The bouncer, or guardian of the gate, was friendly but insisted his job was at risk if he broke this ratio rule. So, ever creative as theatrical types are, we sent the lead actor, who played a character called ManGot and had a bushy beard, back to the theatre to dress up in drag. He returned in a long dress as the bearded lady, and the guardian of the gate just shrugged and laughed and let us in.

These public houses still exist and have a certain historical charm. In fact, I think places like The Brunswick House should be nominated for official UNESCO Heritage Site status—although I guess The Brunswick would be disqualified because of modernization: These places are now unabashedly, unashamedly, co-ed, and old and odd rules such as not carrying your beer to another table to socialize have been discarded. Hell, some of these old pubs now even have lithesome lassies flirting with young macho males. But in the air lingers the oh-so-Canadian priggishness and concern about the danger of mixing drink in mixed company.

Finally, there is that Canuck watering hole called a hotel, for a *hotel* was, contrary to what you might assume, also a drinking establishment. In fact it was the closest to what most people (including Canadians) would now call a bar.

My wife and I had lived in Toronto for less than a month when one of her co-workers called me up one afternoon to tell me that since everyone at the office was quitting early he was "taking her to a hotel downtown after work", and I should join them as soon as I finished work. Ahem! Was such a casual ménage a trios a Canadian folkway? Could he give me the room number? Or should I just ask the desk clerk? (But then I'd need to know whose name they signed on the registry!)

In Robin Hood's England, and still to this day, inns (or in modern idiom, hotels) were places where the weary traveller found both food and drink and a place to rest his weary head. So the inn/hotel was the place that not only weary travellers quaffed their thirst, but also the place the locals went to get away from home and down a few.

So hotels were the third alternative watering holes. Many of these hotels were no longer real hotels, although a good number rented a few rooms on a weekly or monthly basis, perhaps just to grease the wheels of getting a liquor license. In fact in my own town, several of the drinking establishments, including a few that are very rowdy 'bars' catering to the university crowd, are former real hotels that still do rent rooms upstairs to the down and out.

So, the bottom line, for the Yankee visitor to English Canada is that if you want to drink, you'll probably have to search further than back home—unless you're from a dry county—and 'hotel' translates to bar while 'tavern' translates to a restaurant licensed to serve booze with your meal. (Real pubs, public houses, are now few and far between.) It is somewhat ironic, or paradoxical, that the importation of British drinking ways has led to a country where 'locals', the neighbourhood bar where neighbours socialized, never properly evolved, for the local pub in England is as ubiquitous as the local bar in any Yankee city.

Quebec, however, is a different story. They have bars, true 'locals'. They don't restrict the sale of beer to government outlets that are closed when you most want a brew. You can buy beer or wine at any corner store—which are commonly called '*deps*', which is short for *depanneur*s. If you want to pick up a six-pack on the way home from the bar, you can just duck into a 'dep' on your wavering way home. The neighbourhood watering hole is as common as it is in any Chicago neighbourhood. It may be called 'bar' or 'bistro' or 'resto' or any of a number of other names, but no foreign traveller will have any difficulty finding one. It should be said that there are some suburban neighbourhoods that are 'dry', in the sense that they license establishments that are exclusively for drinking. But you can still purchase wine and beer at the corner dep, and rare indeed is any commercial establishment (one that expects you to sit down at a table after you walk in) that won't offer libation.

The other major difference is the friendliness. There is no need to know French to feel totally at home even in the most backwater bar in rural Quebec. Contrary to the stereotype of the French as haughty and aloof, the average Quebecois with a glass of beer or wine in front of him is one contented, amiable guy—or gal—more than willing to socialize with newcomers, even if it has to be by sign language or a game of pool.

Update

Some things have changed. You won't easily find anything called a 'pub' anymore, and thankfully those days when a drinking establishment could set a rule of only allowing entry to women accompanied by a male 'escort' are an historical oddity. And now you can legally carry your drink to another table. (Although don't try to carry it outside the licensed to drink area—not even just outside the establishment's door should you step out to have a smoke.)

The liquor laws generally have gradually become a bit more liberal, and most restaurants other than fast food joints have a liquor license, which in Ontario they prominently display on their signs with the letters LCBO, meaning licensed to serve alcoholic beverages by the Liquor Control Board of Ontario.) But this Puritanical obsession with governmental control of liquor sales and consumption is still characteristic of most of

Canada. Of course, our regulations may actually seem libertine to a Yank from a dry county, but I think most Yanks would find them a bit crazy. (The French certainly would, although the Brits might not.)

Cuisine: The Awful Almost Unpalatable Truth

Yank Question: How does Canadian cuisine differ from American cuisine?

Canuck Answer: American cuisine is just one (albeit major) subcategory of the more varied Canadian cuisine, for, you see, Canucks also have British 'cuisine' (an oxymoron up there with jumbo shrimp and military intelligence) and Québécoise cuisine—i.e., stuff consumed in Quebec. The last mentioned is most important, for we all know how sophisticated French cuisine is! This is to say we not only poison our bodies with Big Macs and sweets, we vary our diets with such Quebecois health foods as Sugar Pie and Poutine.

Sugar Pie is self-explanatory—albeit a bit scary to imagine—and typical of Quebecois fondness for diabetes-inducing stuff. But *poutine*? What's that? Well French cuisine is universally considered one of the great cuisines, and it is a cuisine whose reputation is largely based on its wonderful sauces. Even the sound of their most basic sauces tripping off one's tongue (*Béarnaise, Béchamel, Hollandaise, Rémoulade*) are enough to make any Epicurean's mouth water, and sauce is one of three critical components in poutine.

The second ingredient is cheese. Charles de Gaulle allegedly once responded to the chaotic political situation in his country with the plaintive cry: "How can you govern a country which has three hundred kinds of cheeses?!" (And, incidentally, that number apparently has now doubled, although the Swiss still allegedly have even more varieties—and a more stable government.) The French love cheese—except in their art. (It's Yanks who like cheesy art.) So cheese, a very special cheese, is the second of three components of poutine.

The third ingredient? The base on which the above two ingredients build. Well, right-wing, right-thinking Yanks may know this item by the name "Freedom Fries". When France sensibly refused to participate in the Yankee invasion of Iraq, all things French suddenly became obscene and repugnant in the self-righteous 50. Americans were not going to support those cowardly Frogs by eating *French* fries, but nor were they going give up a basic staple in their diet, so the Congressional cafeteria (and other patriotic eateries) renamed them Freedom Fries. Never big readers or deep thinkers, the thought that a rose (or fry) by any other name…etcetera—never crossed their little minds.

Let me say a few things about French fries before returning to a closer look at the components of poutine. French fries are as central to the diet of both Canucks and Yanks as rice is to the Asian and Near Eastern countries or pasta is to Italy or potatoes in more digestible forms is to the Germanic lands. Nonetheless, calling them *French* fries *may* just be as much a misnomer as 'Freedom Fries'. The Brits call them 'chips' (as in *fish 'n chips*), and call what we North Americans call 'chips'—'crisps'. The origin of this way of preparing potatoes by deep-frying them is disputed. Some authorities say they are Belgian (of all things!) in origin. Others claim they once were called German fries, but (like when France became an 'enemy' by not supporting Bush's aggression in Iraq, so too when Germany in World War II became an enemy, a name change, but *not* a dietary change, was called for. It doesn't really matter, I suppose, for what matters is that they (in various guises, degrees of thickness, crispness or sogginess, greasiness, cholesterol levels) are a popular food item in British and North American and French diets. Why this is so escapes me, for frankly I find fries lacking in any redeeming social value and about as interesting in taste as deep-fried Styrofoam. But I am clearly not typical of my fellow citizens in this.

So back to poutine (pronounced poo-teen, or peuh-tsin). The dish is prepared with a base of French (Belgian, German, Freedom) fries over which is added the cheese and the sauce—ideally in two or more layers. The cheese is—not a Camembert, a Brie, a Chabis Feuille, a Montbriac, a Petit Caprin, a Livarot —but so-called *cheese curds*. Cheese curds are fresh, young white cheddar cheese hunks of random shapes—your basic cheddar cheese before being formed into blocks and properly aged. The connoisseur of cheese curds does not judge this cheese by its taste or 'nose', but by its *squeak*: A really good cheese curd squeaks most audibly when you bite into it. If your dog barks when you sink your teeth in one of these curds, you know you have hit gold. These squeaky curds are almost exclusively available only in Quebec. The reason is that the squeak fades in the first 24 hours after their creation, and only in Quebec are such fresh curds usually available. Now most Canucks are not connoisseurs of course, so in Anglophone Canada the rustic natives will eat poutine made with mozzarella cheese or even (ugh!) more commonly consume 'poutine' without any cheese at all and call it by a different name: "chips and gravy".

Gravy? Huh!? Sorry, but yes well *that* is the traditional 'sauce'. No, not some exotic, rich French sauce imported from Paris, no high-falutin Béchamel or Hollandaise, but rather the stuff you buy in a can called, in down-home, plain-folk language, *gravy*. Oh there is a popular variation called Poutine Italienne which uses spaghetti meat sauce in place of gravy, but that's a foreign corruption. (Damn WOPs!) The purist's poutine uses only plain gravy.

.

I've spent a perhaps excessive amount of words on this poutine dish, but I feel it really is almost archetypal when it comes to understanding my fellow citizens' approach to food. It is exemplary in representing both the similarities and differences between Canuck and Yank cuisine. Let me explain.

.

I think it *is* fair to speak of a general American cuisine, although of course *cuisine* is far too kind a word. The Yankee fast-food, drive-through, chow-down, and bloat-up tradition is well established. MacDonald's and KFC and their ilk are ubiquitous throughout the putatively civilized world—strong evidence of America's effective culinary imperialism. Pizza or Chinese take-out only runners-up, perhaps because coming from the rich and wonderful culinary traditions of Italy and China they actually bear some relationship to real food—and real food it seems has little appeal to the hoi polloi everywhere. Less defensible is to speak of Canadian cuisine as a distinct entity. Quebecoise cuisine, yes, but Canada as a whole is eclectic to the point of anonymity when it comes to any distinctive cuisine. Yanks have their outposts too where distinctive food is prepared; e.g., New Orleans with its Cajun and Creole traditions. But these, like Quebec, are special cases and not definitive of the national taste.

.

If you look for a place to dine in any but the really large Canadian cities, you will find restaurants that claim to offer Canadian and Chinese, and often Italian cuisine, and not much else except U.S. based fast-food joints and pizza places. On the menus of these dining establishments one will find allegedly Canadian chow which is in fact American fast food prepared slowly but not better (burgers, grilled cheese, chicken fingers, etc.). The Italian and Chinese offerings will, however, be legitimate Italian and Chinese dishes, but only the latter, in most cases, close to the real thing. (Canada was stitched together into one nation by the railroad, and the labour was provided by so-called 'coolies': Chinese immigrants many of whom eventually settled in the towns and cities along the stitching and opened restaurants. This is why virtually every whistle-stop, or former whistle-stop, in Canada will have as its one restaurant a place offering "Chinese/Canadian" food.)

So now, given this background, it should be clear why poutine is so symbolic and symptomatic of Canadian cuisine. It's the restaurant staple that in various incarnations distinguishes us. Canucks are a strange mongrel blend of three cultures: Brits, Yanks and Frogs. All three have a weakness for 'fries'. (This is understandable with the Brits and Yanks who were weaned from mother's milk to a diet of bland junk-food, but the French should know better. Maybe they just like to slum once in a while?) Well, for Brits and Yanks and Frogs, fries are a regrettable part of their 'cuisine'. But for Canucks fries are *definitive*—because they represent the Canadian tradition of choosing the worst feature of their three 'motherlands' and making it emblematic of being a Canuck.

Fries with gravy. MacDonald's dry-stick fries doused with vinegar. Greasy Quebecois fries made even more soggy with gravy and then squeaky with cheese curds. We stamp each cultural import with our individual mark.

We'll order fries from one of the ubiquitous Yank fast food chains, but then tag (soak) them with vinegar—a British thing. (That, dear Yankee readers, is the reason those strange vials of vinegar sit on the table of many local restaurants north of the border.) But in deference to our southern neighbours we might just add ketchup. Or we might opt for 'fries and gravy' that pimple fertilizer so popular with Canuck teens.

Or as the ultimate national gesture we might order that poutine thing which combines French love of cheese, Yankee love of gravy, and British love of soggy messes with all three cultures' fondness for 'fries'.

Postscript. Of course I'm being, as is my wont, unfair to everyone in this. Canada, Great Britain and The United States all offer a larger variety of truly fine culinary opportunities than do even most of the countries with great cuisines. It is just that these delights are all imported. Should you want to eat well in any of these countries, you dine at so-called 'ethnic restaurants'. Just do not eat the local stuff—except as a down-and-dirty, go-native research anthropologist's exercise.

Canada's few large cities offer dining experiences (and available foodstuffs) that probably exceed some of the great cities of Europe—where national pride in their native cuisine and less cultural diversity limits the variety of culinary offerings. Toronto, Ottawa and Vancouver are great places to find wonderful dining experiences and exotic foods. All have restaurants offering menus from many and varied lands and great market areas for those willing to experiment at home.

.

And Montreal! Oh Montreal! I am not alone in my view that this is the most cosmopolitan city in the world—and *the* place on the planet for those who love food in all its diversity. Commentators far, far more traveled and experienced than yours truly wax poetic about Montreal. It is Alice's Restaurant: you really can get anything you want! What do you want to eat? Afghan? Algerian? Berber? Cajun? Caribbean? Creole? Croatian? Ethiopian? Greek? Hungarian? Indonesian? Japanese? Korean? Kosher? Lebanese? Mexican? Moroccan? Peruvian? Polish? Portuguese? Russian? Salvadorian? Slovenian? Spanish? Thai? Turkish? Vietnamese? And of course every variety of Chinese, Italian, and French. Oh, just stick a pin in a world map and go to Montreal's Yellow pages.

.

Now you may be able, if your palate is more sophisticated than mine (admittedly not too difficult), be able to get a Frenchie meal in France that you find superior to any in Montreal—even in the Old Port area. But the point is that in even most of the most cosmopolitan European countries, and especially in those with an exceptional national cuisine, the diversity of eating opportunities is more limited than it is in Montreal. Montreal is all of Europe packed into one compact city where virtually any culinary delight is within walking distance.

.

Postscript 2. One absolutely distinctive dish no one who ever travels to Montreal should miss is Montreal Smoked Meat. There is an ongoing, often acrimonious, debate as to where the best smoked meat resides—with Schwartz's, I believe, currently holding the title. But nowhere outside of Quebec is there anything, no matter how falsely labeled, which is *real* Montreal Smoked Meat. Accept no substitutes.

.

Postscript 3. I may be forgetting for what readership this is intended. Yanks, fear not! You can find a MacDonald's, a Harvey's, a Burger King, a KFC, a Pizza Hut or whatever is your preference in junk comfort-food in most cities of population over 10,000. You'll also find the standard "bar & grill" chain restaurants (e.g., Casey's and Kelsey's) with menus indistinguishable from those found in their equivalent establishments south of the border. And, failing that, when you see any restaurant that advertises Canadian cuisine, rest assured it'll be your native stuff—only difference being that vial of vinegar that may be sitting on the table to sog your fries and make the salt stick.

Update

Here not really much has changed, other than the once ubiquitous vinegar dispenser on the table, which is becoming rare. I live in a community of about 50,000 folks, but our restaurant choices still remain absurdly limited. Occasionally an ethnic restaurant will open, but it rarely survives more than a year.

So my wife and I don't dine out often, for why do so if the food is ordinary? Plus eating out is ridiculously expensive. This is especially true of any place that permits having a drink with your your meal, because the price for any alcoholic drink is often 3 times what it costs even at our over-priced, 'licensed' liquor stores. The good news is the variety of foods available at a supermarket continues to increase greatly. You may not be able to find an ethnic restaurant, but you can find even the most unusual critical ingredients at the store.

Dining Out: A Survival Guide

Yank Question: How does one find a good restaurant in Canada?

Canuck Answer: Visit Quebec.

Supplementary Yank Question: How does one find a good restaurant in English Canada?

Canuck Answer: Find a new immigrant and discreetly shadow him until he enters some eating establishment.

I know the last answer raises yet another Yank Question: how do you spot a new immigrant? Well, the best way is to find two people together and then eavesdrop on their conversation. If it ain't English, or at least if it is sprinkled with non-English phrases, you're set. And be careful: immigrants from England usually speak something that sounds foreign to Yanks; you most certainly don't want to follow *them* to an eatery.

But first things first: Quebec.

As the previous chapter should have made abundantly clear, traditional Quebecois food is very, very different from that of France. Sugar pie and poutine, just like burgers and Kraft Dinner in The States, may be comfort food and very popular with their indigenous peoples, but these are not dishes that will get their countries nominated to any culinary hall of fame. I'm a pleb and a peasant myself, and I like a really good burger from some greasy Yankee spoon, and will admit to finding sugar pie just the thing to fuel me up on a cold Canuck winter day. I'm no food critic with exquisitely refined taste, as God (and my family) knows. However, though my taste and taste buds may be as blunt as my prose, I think I can offer a bit of advice about dining out in my adopted land.

My first piece of advice about dining out in Canada is that Quebec is the place to do it. The reason is not poutine or sugar pie. The reason is that I confuse Montreal with Quebec. And Montreal is the place to dine out.

Montreal is the most cosmopolitan city I've ever visited—and this is especially true of the myriad variety of foods available there—in stores and in restaurants. New York is famous for its diversity of restaurants, but far more knowledgeable folk than me agree with me that it places behind Montreal. And what about Europe? Paris? Rome? London? (Well, forget I even mentioned London.) European cities, naturally enough, specialize in their own local cuisine, and also have a good number of restaurants offering the culinary delights of their homeland. Well, while local Quebec cuisine is not anything to write home to Julia Child about, Montreal has at least as great a diversity of immigrants as New York—and certainly more than most European cities. That is why it is—as I've said already—truly, literally, Alice's Restaurant where you can get anything you want.

Having said that and having already ranted about Canuck cuisine in general, let me turn now to the experience of dining out in Canada. It can sometimes be a stressful experience.

Analyze, break down, the major components that comprise the dining out experience. Well, I can think of, in no specific priority order, five things: 1) the selection available; 2) the food; 3) the ambience and comfort; 4) the service; and 5) the cost. I'll deal with these in this rather haphazard order.

Selection available. Well, no surprise, big city beats small town. And, as I've already said Montreal is Cuisine Queen. I've said enough about this matter already, but I should add that some unlikely places such as Kingston, Ontario, can surprise one with great 'ethnic' restaurants. There is a good book called *Where To Eat In Canada* by Anne Hardy and published by Oberon Press that is worth looking at. In it you'll find some 'ethnic' surprises in unlikely places.

The food. Again I don't want to repeat myself, but I do want to add a few remarks about how to make an educated guess as to where to eat in the average Canuck town. Most travellers probably know the urban myth that to eat where the truckers eat is a good bet. Actually it is a very bad bet. To follow the locals, not the transients with trucks, is better advice. My own town has a local pizza place that I think was opened by the first Europeans (apparently from Italy?!) to land on our shores. (Okay, I exaggerate: Greco's was originally founded as a bakery in 1913 by Oscar Greco.) It remains the compass point of the whole city, and is one of the best eateries in town serving much more than pizza—although their pizza is truly exceptional. And, of course, if in Toronto, Montreal or Vancouver, one needs no advice other than to avoid restaurants that 'specialize' (ahem) in "American/Canadian/Chinese" cuisine.

The ambience and comfort. Well, these are probably as varied as in America, except for the greater willingness of Canadian dining establishments to tolerate loitering. I'd like to think this is some European influence that somehow seeped into our culture. But don't expect full European ambience! Two very undesirable traits we share with at least some of our southern neighbours are absurd attitudes toward smoking, dogs, and children. Except for Quebec (and at the time of this writing this has just changed even there—among the infamously chain-smoking Frogs) lighting up in a restaurant (and even a bar!) is a no-no. In Ontario the environment is polluted and defaced everywhere with ugly signs threatening a $5,000 fine for anyone so delinquent as to take a puff on the latest incarnation of the evil weed. (I'm not kidding! You'd get off easier for grand larceny.) The Ontario government just budgeted 5 million (!) dollars to fund smoke police to enforce this draconian law. My son, who has been living in Central Europe for more than half a decade, tells his Lithuanian or Slovak or Slovenian or Czech or Russian bar buddies this, and they refuse to believe him: they find it too absurd. He must be pulling their legs. Of course this puritanical craziness (justified by dubious science about second-hand smoke) has done serious damage to the restaurant and bar industry. But whoa, I'm a smoker, and obviously biased, so I won't stand on this soap box any longer. Suffice it to say: if you'd like a cig while you wait for your meal or long for one with your coffee afterwards, you should in Canada expect to have to go outside like a pariah and (during most of our year) freeze your cookies off as you quickly feed your lungs your chosen poison. This is not what I consider a fine start or finish to a relaxing dining out experience! But of course, Yanks are used to this already.

.

Another very unEuropean and very uncivilized prohibition is that against kids and dogs. This exists many places down south too, but in Canada, except Quebec, it is virtually universal. Again, I must confess a bias here. Not only do I smoke, but I've had kids and I still have dogs—all three things which I value, although, admittedly, I might just trade one of my kids (but not one of my dogs!) for a pack of smokes when I'm having a nicotine fit.

.

A few anecdotes to illustrate.

.

My three-year old Labrador Retriever could pass as a service dog; he is so well-behaved. But unless I put on dark glasses, borrow a white cane and walk him on harness rather than conventional collar (and I *have* considered this disguise), he is not permitted to sit next to me on even an outdoor (!) patio. (Except in Quebec.) He's a health hazard, allegedly.

The drunk at the next table spitting blood is okay, but my Nicky is a health hazard? And of course in Ontario, the profound fear that someone should venture outside the perimeter of "Place That Allows Drinking" has resulted in most bar and restaurant patios having miniature Berlin Walls set up to keep the clientele from escaping out and contaminating the outside environment. So when traveling with my canine buddy, it is difficult to find even a patio where I can quarantine him on the sidewalk near enough for him to see me through the patio bars. Once, walking my dog in the wee morning hours in Niagara Falls, I tried to walk in the door of a tiny, deserted coffee shop to order a coffee with Nick politely at my side. The counter was at most three feet inside the door. The waitress or proprietor almost had an apoplectic fit. I had to back out and call my request to her. She carried my coffee out to me and then carried my loonie (that's a Canuck buck) back in.

.

And kids? Well, another anecdote. My city hosts a so-called Heritage Festival every summer. This no longer consists of anything whatsoever to do with the city's heritage. Instead they bring in an air show, including (typically) such unpleasant flying creatures as the American Stealth Bomber, and a few has-been rock groups. For this fun festival they fence in a large part of the waterfront where people normally take their kids and dogs to play all summer. You can gain admittance to this fun fortress by paying an exorbitant sum of cash and having a wrist bracelet attached which you cannot remove for three days—unless you want to cough up cash again. As is, alas, only too typical of Canuck attitudes toward folks gathering together to have fun, as you approach the 'grounds' and the giant fence you are informed that dogs, bikes, skateboards, shirtless guys, and anyone carrying food or drink—especially drink worth drinking—are forbidden entrance. They will let kids in, but…

.

The night of one of the concerts, which I had brought my young nieces visiting from Indiana to see (Shaggy! Yikes!) I was sitting at a table at the one—yes one!—place in the whole fair grounds where it was possible to have a beer while they listened to Mister Lover Lover preen and prance and praise himself on stage. A father, with his three or four year old son in tow, arrived at the entrance gate to a secured area. This place serves food, but the kitchen was closed for the night, so the bouncer, the guardian of the gate, told Dad that he couldn't bring his little boy into this den of iniquity where maybe a dozen grownups were having a beer while their teenagers grooved to Shaggy's pseudo-music sexual innuendos.

.

I hasten to add this would not happen in Quebec. Nor, of course, anywhere in Europe I've ever been.

Service. In Canada it is good and polite. I, and I think most of my countrymen (and women), are appalled at Yankee rudeness, especially when it comes from those who are allegedly paid to serve you. (Of course, Canadians are also startled by the casual Yankee friendliness, which I think some find a bit intrusive. Few are the Canadian waitresses who will call you "honey" or "sweetie". It seems a bit intimate and presumptuous doesn't it, to call a total stranger "sweetie"?) And I don't think I've ever heard a server in this country say, at least within hearing range of a patron, a four-letter word. But in my travels and travails back in my land of origin, I have, more than once and for no good reason, been verbally abused by someone who is being paid to serve me. And generally I think it is fair to say that Yanks are more in need of having their mouths washed out with soap than Canucks.

Cost. The cost of eating out is roughly equivalent in my experience. Of course the ever fluctuating exchange rate will determine whether it's cheaper or more expensive for one from the north to eat at home or down south—and vice versa. But in the frame of reference of income within either country, eating out takes approximately the same size bite from the family income pie. What is different is the range. Reflecting the greater discrepancy between haves and have-nots in The States the *range* of prices paid to eat out is greater. There are few, probably no, restaurants in Canada that will top off your meal with the kind of tab you might find on your plate at *Masa* in NYC ($300-500 *prix-fixe*) or numerous other up-up-upscale dining establishments in the Big Apple or LA or D.C. But at the other end of the spectrum, you probably can eat cheaper (albeit not better) in some of the American fast-food chains and local greasy spoons than you can anywhere in Canada.

So the bottom line? Canada isn't that very different from The States when it comes to the 'dining out experience'. We're just more consistent, less extreme, more polite, and probably a bit more uptight about drinking, smoking, kids and dogs. But even that generalization depends on the particular U.S. location to which Canada is being compared. I hear tell Montana is pretty laid back and Kansas so squeaky clean, it's as squeaky as a good cheese curd.

Update

The major change is that the uptight attitude toward smoking, dogs, and kids has worsened everywhere. This is even true of Quebec, although it still remains less uptight than English Canada. Unfortunately this North American attitude has even spread to the countries in the European Union, so it isn't just Canada and the U.S. that are being homogenized.

Oh, and the reference to Greco's in North Bay is obsolete. Their food and their rep has gone way downhill.

Sex, Drugs and Rock 'n Roll

Now we get to the juicy parts. Or do we? I have the impression that most Yanks think Canucks are tough, beer-swilling, macho hockey enforcers—and somehow at the same time swishy, fag-loving, pagan perverts. Well, consistency has never been a strong point of our southern neighbours' justification for their xenophobia. Or maybe, I'll admit, my impression is wrong. Still, I'm sure that the Bible Belt Boys think we're seriously twisted—what with this gay marriage thing. And I also remember how the few Canadian guys at my university in Chicago had a rep for being tough guys—a rep, incidentally, that got them a lot of dates.

And then there is our apparently laissez faire attitude toward drugs: Yet another reason to watch more closely that "longest unguarded border in the world" both countries were once bragging about. Now Yank vigilantes, concerned that our famously good B.C. bud is making its way across this 4,000 mile (i.e., 6,437 kilometre, as we say up here) unguarded border and undermining the noble American "War On Drugs", are trying to patrol this border.

Well, again, the reality doesn't match up all that well with either stereotype. Few of us Canucks are nearly as tough as the toughs in the tough, big city ghettos south of the border. And we can be just as bigoted about homosexuals as any southern Bible thumper. As far as being sexually 'liberal', I'd say on average, yes, we are more so—but in theory more than in practice, more so in tolerance than in actual behaviour. And drugs? Well, I'll deal with that as soon as my dealer shows up.

Sex: Beats Three Dogs In The Tent To Keep Warm

Yank Question: Your former Prime Minster Trudeau said something about the government having no place in the bedrooms of the nation? What did he mean?

Canuck Answer: Take no offence! He intended no innuendo about any of the few recent U.S. Presidents who reputedly have had sex. He simply meant his cabinet ministers should stop hitting on his young wife, Margaret.

I get the impression that many Americans think Canucks are libertines for whom anything goes. I mean *really*: an annual Gay Pride parade in Toronto where nearly naked young men dressed in scanty women's clothing strut down Queen (note the name) Street wiggling their muscular buttocks at spectators! (Obviously most Americans have never been to New Orleans, if this strikes them as foreign decadence.)

But never mind that, Canuck sodomites are dealt with in the next section; let's talk about understanding the basic, heterosexual attitudes toward sex. Basic *sex*. Having sex. Its value. Its socially redeeming value. (Canadians are very big on socially redeeming values.)

Now, Yanks are clearly divided on the issue of sex—with some pro (on the east and west coast) and many con (filling up the bulging middle of America). I don't think we up here are as polarized. We all pay lip service (no *double entendre* intended) to its 'value', but we are hardly what could be called hedonistic. We like our sex sanitized and politically correct.

The politically correct streak in Canucks often exceeds even that of Yanks. (I know this is hard to believe!) For example, Toronto (once appropriately called "Toronto The Good" because of its squeaky clean reputation) recently banned a popular, very bland, middle-of-the-road, pop group from playing in its City Hall square because of their name—"The Bare Naked Ladies". (The band is all male and performs fully clothed.) And also recently Miss Universe, who is a Toronto native, was only allowed to do a public appearance there if any reference to her as Miss Universe was avoided because, of course, beauty pageants are politically incorrect, and her physical attributes being reason for admiration just ain't right. This, remember, is the city that annually holds a huge pageant and parade for homosexuals, where the gay boys are quite explicit in displaying their charms. Of course, Canadians, like Americans, are nothing if not inconsistent.

So this should give one an idea about how contradictory my fellow citizens' attitudes are when it comes to matters of sex. This inconsistency differs from that of our southern neighbours in that it often exists *within the same segment of the population.* It is admittedly a simplification, but a useful one, to divide the U.S. of A. into two different cultures. On one hand there is the East and West Coast, and on the other hand there is Middle America. Of course New York City and California are radically different in many respects and often engage in cultural wars (including 'gansta rap' wars), but they do have much more in common with each other than with Middle America. So when speaking of my country's attitudes toward sex, some will undoubtedly seem wildly libertine and decadent to Middle America's allegedly moral majority (which, as an amusing graffito I once saw pointed out, is *neither*), while The Coasters might even think we are actually quite repressed when it comes to sexual matters.

Anyway here is the skinny (the bare facts) on public and private sex in The Land Of The Maple Leaf.

Private. We have the same ongoing war about provincial versus federal rights that Yanks have regarding states versus federal rights. But when it comes to legislation regarding what consenting adults may or may not do to—or with—each other in the privacy of their bedrooms (laundry rooms, dens, bathrooms, root cellars) the federal government (thanks to former Prime Minister Trudeau) has laid (no pun intended) down the law: Do whatever the fuck (no pun intended) you want. Canada, unlike some of The States in the putative Land of Liberty, does not think one should go to jail for engaging in anal or oral sex—or for getting it on with someone with similarly designed genitalia. Gosh, what a radical concept!

No doubt, this will shock and awe Middle Americans from the Bible Belt—but might just do something for our tourism industry, especially from Kansas. As for The Coasters, I suspect it might just earn a shrug.

I should say something about the effects this libertine attitude has had on public morals (actually sexual mores) in my country. Recent statistics—

and yes I know how much to trust 'recent statistics'—indicate that Canucks cheat on their spouses less than Yanks, are less likely to be child-molesters, rapists, and other unsavoury sexual predators than their southern neighbours, and generally are the sort of folk you wouldn't mind having for dinner or letting your daughter date. So I would think (I can't speak from extensive experience on this topic) that the actual sexual behaviour of Canucks is probably on average very similar to that of Yanks, and will vary within the standard range, with most folks in the middle. Certainly most Canadians in bed bear (bare?) more relationship to Americans than to the Irish inhabitants of Ines Beag where tongue kissing or hand stimulations of the penis are strictly *verboten* or, on the other 'hand', to the lucky, lascivious Mozambique Magaians where tradition has boys who are colliding with puberty routinely introduced to the pleasures of sexual intercourse by experienced older women—often relatives or friends of the parents. (And I hope better looking than *my* aunts.)

There are of course geographical correlations with sexual attitudes just as there are in The States, but they are a little more complicated. Our closest analog to Middle America may be the Prairies—although Ontario has a Bible Belt as well. You're not going to find quite the easy-going attitude toward the varieties of sexual experience in Saskatoon, Moose Jaw, or Grand Prairie that you'll find in Vancouver on the west coast or in Montreal. British Columbia seems very much like California in its hippy-dippy, flakey approach to everything—including sex. Montreal, and the Quebecois in general, but to a more restrained degree, have sexual attitudes and behaviour patterns which are typically French, so are probably most distinct. However, overall this general rule is true in most places: the bigger the community, the more diversity and the more diversity is accepted. E.g., you're more likely to find a soul mate who likes to dress up in Daffy Duck costumes and suck your elbows to orgasm in Toronto (or New York) or Vancouver (especially) than in Beavertail, Saskatchewan.

But I should leave this topic alone (i.e., shut up), for being a monogamous guy, I really can only speak from hearsay and circumstantial evidence. For all I *really* know, most Canadians, even those in Beavertail, Saskatchewan once alone with the object of their desire smear themselves with bear grease and invite the family pet in for an orgy.

Public. I can speak with more authority here, as could anyone who read our books and newspapers and watched our films—*and* travelled the country, checking out not only the art galleries, dining spots, and museums, but also the local strip clubs.

Perhaps because of the French influence, and even perhaps partially because of the British concern with freedom of expression, I think most Yanks will find Canucks less puritanical. When I first arrived in Toronto back in 1968, I was shocked (and delighted) to see full frontal nudity on the tube while watching a grown-up film. (If memory serves, which it sometimes doesn't, it was *IF*.) Now we are *not* Europeans—who generally have a more mature, sensible attitude about such matters—but we are certainly closer to them than most Yanks. Europeans found comical the hullabaloo about what's-her-name showing her tit at the Super Bowl game. Well, most Canadians of my acquaintance also thought the Yankee reaction rather ridiculous.

The simple fact is that, in general, Family Values U.S. of A. has a pretty neurotic attitude toward sexuality. I can say this, not withstanding recent trends toward great sexual explicitness and innuendo on Yank TV. There remains something fundamentally adolescent about this apparent loosening of censorship regarding sex. Anything sexual seems to be accompanied by an implied snigger. Public expression of sexual content south of our border strikes me as, alas, almost always vulgar and *very unsexy*. Except insofar as Canadians buy into any changes in Yank culture, most of us up here not quite as crass and unsophisticated.

Of course, we have our own *issues*. These have a lot to do with political correctness—a national pandemic—and with our obsession with being a gentle, polite, clean people. Perhaps the best way to exemplify this is to talk about strip clubs.

Strip clubs are widely accepted, or at least tolerated, in most towns big enough to parade as cities. And nobody seems to make a big deal of their existence. In fact, until not too, too long ago many an ordinary 'family' bar would offer an exotic dancer show just on Friday and Saturday nights. This is a bit like the 'locals' in Prague which normally were unpretentious watering holes for the working class, but once every week would give the usual robust matronly waitresses a night off and replace them with long-limbed, lithe, and nearly naked young women who had contracted to work this working class circuit. The Czech patrons, being Czechs, seemed almost not to notice this temporary staff change—which was never announced ahead of time, as far as I could tell, nor seemed really to do much to increase patronage.

I don't mean to imply my countrymen and women are as grown up as Europeans regarding matters sexual. And also and alas, times have changed, and my Ontario city of 55,000 now only supports two strip clubs, and they are exclusively that—strip clubs. One is downright upscale and one—well, its nickname tells the story: The Swamp. I have to confess that I'm no longer really up-to-speed on the protocols at these places, because of age, annoyance with smoking bans, and a—perhaps (God Forbid!) slightly puritanical and Canadian—distaste for the blurring of the distinction between the visual and the tactile.

But even if my data are out-dated to some extent, I think it offers some insight into the Canuck mentality. I don't think most Canadians feel there is anything particularly socially deviant about going to a strip club. My wife was amused at an anthropology professor at our university who wore his Swamp t-shirt to class—a long throw from lecturing in one's academic gowns. And when I was younger, the Friday afternoon research projects in our department would always be topped off by profs and students heading out together to have a few beer and watch young women take their clothes off. Even the female students came along—to make snide remarks. It was no big deal.

Canadian males watching strippers or 'peelers' (who of course prefer the more dignified appellation 'exotic dancers') are so, so Canadian in their demeanour! No one speaks out of turn or yells obscenities or tries to climb on stage and molest the young women. Over the years I've had at least half a dozen of these women in my classes, and have talked to them (off the job) about their experiences at this work-your-way-through-school part-time employment. Most of them are discreet about what they do when not hitting the books, but most of them just chuckle about the profs they occasionally see in 'perverts row' (the term for the seating by the stage), and their fellow male students whom they inevitably encounter in the clubs. None have told me any horror stories about this life of degradation. Yes, there are drugs, of course, and, yes, a few of the dancers do moonlight as hookers, and, yes, biker gangs and some very sleazy folk are the ones handling business, but overall they made it sound like a safer job than working at an all-night convenience store—certainly so if that store is in a major American city.

As I say, things have changed: these bars would offer something more than the stage show, but it was pretty tame. One could get up one's nerve and ask a dancer whose attributes particularly entranced you for a 'table dance'. This meant, should she agree, that she would come over to your beer-slopped table and gyrate naked close to you for the length of a pop tune (usually three short minutes) for five bucks. But no one ever dared *touch* the dancer. That was *verboten* and the bouncers were very firm about this rule. This is *so* Canadian: polite in our lust. Look, but don't touch.

Of course now it's so-called 'VIP rooms' and private lap dances and, I'm told, touching and more. But I'm sure the same Canuck "please and thank you" mentality operates even here. One thing that always seemed profoundly unsexy to me was the allegedly easy-going, almost too healthy, sexual attitudes of the Swedes. We, other Northerners, seem to have a tinge of that as well. Something about the climate?

Be that as it may, Canadian sexual attitudes and behaviour are in fact a blend of Nordic and French, and that is certainly not a bad mix. I don't think we have anything to compare to the somewhat scary sex clubs one might find in NYC or LA, but nor do we suffer from the even more scary sexual phobia that seems to be endemic in Middle America.

Update

Only changes I can say I've noticed since this was written is both countries becoming a bit less uptight and more tolerant. I can't even report on strip clubs, because my age must be having an effect, much as I'd like to deny it. I haven't visited one in years.

Homosexuality: Queer Views On 'Queers'

Yank Question: What kind of country permits deviants to marry each other?

Canuck Answer: Most countries. I don't know of any that require newlyweds to sign an agreement to limit their sexual behaviour to whatever is the current average for the culture.

Supplementary Question: You know what I mean—homosexuals, legalizing 'gay' marriages.

Canuck Answer: There are two possible answers. One, the kind of country that seriously values a human's right to bond with whomever they like in holy (or unholy, for that matter) matrimony. Two, the kind of country that likes to be at the forefront of the latest trends in political correctness.

I'd like to think the right—or at least the more correct answer—is the former, but I'm sure the latter (leftist) is a big factor. However, it should be noted that the recent move to legalize same-sex marriage has met with considerable resistance by a substantial portion of the Canuck public. The major difference up here is that most folk don't their knickers in a knot about the issue, even if they don't particularly like the idea. We have our religious fundamentalists too, but not nearly as many—and nor are they anywhere near *as* rabidly fundamentalist, and they are not as organized and influential in government policy.

As a practising heterosexual (practice, I'm told, makes perfect), I really am in no position (no pun intended) to say much about the 'gay scene' in Canada. I can say, however, that it isn't a big deal up here and not nearly as emotional an issue as it seems to me below the 49th. All our major cities have a gay community. Montreal's 'gay village', an area just east of downtown, is perhaps the most well known, although I've been told by those in the know that Toronto is considered the Canadian equivalent of San Francisco as a relatively safe, and well-populated, harbour for homosexuals.

However, despite the publicity that Toronto's Gay Pride Parade and recent legislation to legalize same-sex marriage gets, Canada is not

Holland and Toronto is not Amsterdam. (Allegedly more than 50% of the residents of downtown Amsterdam are homosexual or bisexual.) The typical American tourist first visiting Amsterdam will be freaked out by not only the infamous red light district (the premier, must-visit, tourist site for most visitors), but also by the flamboyant and flagrant and laid-back sexual ambience of the whole city. This is not an experience any Yank tourist can expect when visiting Toronto—or even Montreal.

As with so many things, Canadians just don't make quite the big deal that Yanks do about such matters as sexual orientation. I'm sure anyone with *any* somewhat different sexual tendencies has a hard time in small town Canada, just as they would in Pleasantville, Kansas. And be just as happy to find community in Montreal as in NYC.

Update

The Yank's attitudes and laws have changed more dramatically than ours have. Gay marriage is being legalized in many states, albeit not without Puritanical outrage fuelling legal battles to have that legalization revoked.

And being openly gay is now more socially acceptable in both countries, although it's still a big deal when some star athlete 'comes out of the closet'. And some universities even offer courses in "Queer Studies", for the word has largely lost its pejorative connotation.

This is not to say the prejudice and bigotry has universally decreased. But the power of "political correctness' and the sometimes dire consequences of saying anything deemed politically incorrect has disguised the extent of it.

One difference between the two countries that remains is that there is less regional discrepancy within Canada. Rural and urban Canucks differ in their **views far less than rural and urban Yanks.**

The Straight Dope: Oxymoron For A Canuck Druggie

Yank Question: What's with this legalizing of marijuana thing? Don't Canadians want to join us in 'The War On Drugs'?

Canuck Answer: Hell, no!

Generally speaking, I'm proud to say that Canadians are usually quite reluctant to join the U.S. in its stupid, vicious wars, be they on drugs or commies or oil rich countries. In 1939 Germany invaded Poland and days later World War II began. Within a week Canada joined Great Britain and France in the war against fascism. I'm a pacifist, but if there ever was a justifiable war it was World War II. And, hmm, it seems the Yanks waited a couple years until some of their own property (Pearl Harbour) on one of their 'colonies' (it wasn't a state then) was attacked before they deigned to join this conflict. Alas, such reticence to wage war is atypical of American foreign policy since.

Most educated people outside the U. S. of A. can't help but shake their heads in disbelief over the American obsession with waging war on something—*anything*! After they joined World War II, which did much to lift the country out of the doldrums of the Great Depression, being at war against something became national policy. Hell, it not only was good for the economy, it kept the rabble focused on something other than the real ills that plagued the country—such as the appalling gap between "the haves" and "the have nots". It must be admitted that this highly pragmatic policy *is* effective, for the rabble remains distracted from the country's real ills to this day—even as this gap between rich and poor increases exponentially.

After WWII, with the Nazis and fascists defeated, a new war was declared (the so-called 'cold war') against the boogie man of communism. This is not to imply communism wasn't a real evil, only that the motives (e.g., greed) and actual practices (e.g., McCarthyism) of these cold warriors were dubious to say the least. In fact this new war almost resulted in the virtual annihilation of the human race in the incredibly high-stakes political pissing contest we now call the 'Cuban Missile Crisis'. And then, ironically, the real evil of Soviet fascism collapsed under its own bureaucratic weight and corruption rather than because of the proliferation of weapons of mass destruction in America. But with communism a dead issue after 1989, as the Berlin Wall was torn down, and one by one all those Soviet satellite countries escaped from the Kremlin's orbit, the America government and the military-industrial complex was left without a unifying enemy to distract its populace from deteriorating conditions at home.

Hmm. One can imagine the brainstorming session. "We need an enemy." "Well, the country is a violent mess, and we can't outright blame the poor who commit most of the crimes. But, hey, most of them use drugs to ease the pain of their daily lives. Let's blame drugs. Yes, let's have a War On Drugs!"

In my hometown in Northern Ontario we have a NORAD base. When communism went down the sewer it belonged in, this base was given a new mission: spot, not Soviet missiles, but planes sneaking nasty drugs into North America. But despite the Canadian government's complicity in this silliness, most Canadians were just as unwilling to be allies in this 'war' as they were regarding the Vietnam debacle.

Readers may by now be detecting a pattern. Canadians just don't get so worked up about things as Americans. I may be flattering Canadians, but maybe, just maybe, this is because we aren't so simple-minded and single-minded.

According to "Marijuana Arrests and Incarceration in the United States: Preliminary Report" by Chuck Thomas there "were more than 695,201 marijuana arrests in the United States in 1997. This was the largest number in U.S. history. Of these arrests, 87.2% were for possession—not sale or manufacture. There have been more than 11 million marijuana arrests in the United States since 1965. There are an estimated 15,668 people presently incarcerated in federal prisons for marijuana offences, comprising about 12.7% of the total federal prison population." This is an old report, but my casual, admittedly unscholarly research, indicates things have only gotten worse.

If these data don't disturb you, you probably should throw this book away—if you haven't already. This is nuts. It is *so* nuts, I can't even begin to comment on it without stammering. In 1920, America instituted Prohibition and maintained it for 13 years. In doing so they virtually created organized crime syndicates—and did nothing to prevent excessive alcohol consumption. In fact, because beer (the perceived evil) was more difficult to produce than hard liquor, prohibition actually led to more people becoming real alcoholics. All the evidence that Prohibition was a disastrous example of social engineering ("The Noble Experiment" it was called) is so old, so well documented, that I won't waste any more words reiterating it.

.

It is equally obvious that the current version of Prohibition is just as socially destructive. I won't get into the 'juicer' versus 'doper' debate about whether alcohol or marijuana is more hazardous to your health and the health of those around you. Cirrhosis of the liver ain't good, but a single joint has as much tar as a pack of smokes. Drunk drivers are a bad thing, but stoned drivers aren't any better. That is not the issue. The simple fact is that crimes without victims should not be crimes, and no naïve well-intentioned social engineers, no warriors against drugs, no vice squads, no "Just say No" slogan campaigns are going to change the reality that human beings will use recreational drugs. (And some will abuse them.) This is a universal behaviour of *homo sapiens*. Ask your neighbourhood anthropologist.

.

Most civilized countries in the world acknowledge this fact, this human 'weakness'—which may actually be a socially useful safety valve. There are no Liquor Control Boards in Tahiti. And in most places in the world, having a toke on a joint wouldn't land you in jail. It seems the average Yank has a bee in his bonnet and a pickle up his butt about marijuana, which, alas, is a sad case of history repeating itself. Canadians emulate their neighbours to the south—and worry excessively about alienating them. But to our credit, we don't make criminals of our teenagers, or imprison them as felons, for inhaling a particular kind of smoke that gives them the munchies and the giggles.

.

And, I should add, serious destructive drug abuse and the organized (and disorganized) crime associated with it, while a serious problem everywhere, including Canada, is far less a problem in Canada and other countries with more liberal laws regarding drugs than it is in the United States of America.

.

Caveat: this doesn't mean we have Amsterdam-style cafes where you can sit and read the newspaper while smoking a joint. And it would be unwise to try to bring any home-grown (inferior) American weed across the Peace Bridge into Canada. Canada is reaching a reasonable level of tolerance, but we're hardly an anything-goes drug culture. We even have, alas, narcs!

.

And, sadly, the decriminalization of marijuana possession legislation, at time of writing, is being withdrawn by the newly elected Conservative Party, which has sucking up to the Bush Administration as a major priority.

Update

In 2013 two states legalized marijuana, although the federal government still considers possession illegal, and the well-funded DEA narcs still waste time and ruin lives by persecuting pot smokers. But at least some regions of the U.S. are pulling ahead of Canada, for we still haven't decriminalized it.

However, certainly the general public's tolerance of using this particular inebriant has gradually increased. President Clinton admitted to 'trying it', but claimed that he "didn't inhale". President Obama wasn't as absurdly coy.

Yet Canucks seem to still be more tolerant in general than Yanks. The walking disaster who is the current major of Toronto, Rob Ford, has been video-taped smoking crack with some really sleazy crack dealers, and his good buddy is a dope dealer. Not only hasn't he been charged with anything, he hasn't lost his job as major of Canada's largest city. Furthermore, he is running for re-election with enough electoral support that he could quite possibly win. (I know this doesn't say much for Canadian intelligence.)

Rock 'n Roll Out The Carpet: It's Legal In Canada

Yank Question: Is music piracy really legal in Canada, and what kind of music is popular up in there in the frozen North?

Canuck Answer: That's two questions! And there is no simple answer to either.

I'll keep this short—partially because things are changing so rapidly and I'd like to finish this book before it becomes outdated because of a U.S. takeover of Canada.

First: is music and video piracy legal? No, not exactly. The amount of Internet file-sharing per capita going on is probably about the same here as it is in The States, but I don't have any statistics. But here it has not, as of writing this, yet been made an illegal activity. It is illegal to upload 'pirated' material if one knows it is pirated, but proving such knowledge is damn difficult. It is not illegal to share your legitimately purchased tunes. I won't say whether this is or is not a good thing, for that is one debate I do not wish to enter into. I will say I believe the reason that it is still legal here in Canada has nothing to do with the morality of it. It is simply because The Hollywood Empire and The Yank Music Industry don't have as much clout in Parliament as they do in Congress, nor, because we have only one-tenth the population, is our behaviour as important to them. Right now those Canadians who are prone to paranoia do not have to worry that some monolithic 'entertainment industry' will send goons to their house to check out their computers for 'illegal' mp3 copies of the latest Britney Spears atonal masterpiece—which will have a street value a few years from now of approximately the value of a politician's promise. The average teenager in Canada is not sitting in his bedroom downloading the Backstreet Boys while looking out the window to be sure no cop car is pulling up. (It's hard to flush a hard drive down the toilet when the cops show up!) Canuck kids just download the same crap—free of paranoia.

Which brings me to the second question. The kind of music that is popular up here is the same kind of music that is popular down below. Not only the same kind: the same music. But this is a topic for a later chapter. Suffice it to say, that no Yank is going to tune to a Canadian AM station upon crossing the border and suddenly be exposed to throat singing or Eskimo folk song.

.
.
.

Update

.

Actually, despite what I expected, things haven't changed that much. So-called 'piracy' is now technically illegal in both countries, and still common. But it can be risky in The States, where the big movie and music companies seem to enjoy making an example of some randomly chosen kid who gets caught downloading too many hit movies or pop songs.

Palisade Park Politics

American politics is really not very complicated, at least in the broad outline. Two parties. One is slightly to the left on the political spectrum if you call the centre a place much further right than most civilized countries do. The other is just right of Attila the Hun. I came to Canada with this nice neat little packaged view of politics. I was, of course, being young, a leftie who felt the Democrats lacked *cajones*, but the Republicans were devils incarnate. (Lord knows, I'm not really a 'leftie' anymore, but I still think this evaluation is not far off the mark.) So, typical Yank, I tried to superimpose my simplistic view on the far more complex Canadian political system. At the time Canada had these three major political parties: The Liberals, The Conservatives, and The New Democrats. Three parties! Hmm, that was odd, but applying my equation as best I could, I decided Liberal equalled Democrat and Conservative equalled Republican and … well the NDP was a socialist, social justice party, something inconceivable in my Fatherland!

Ah, the naiveté of youth! It's hard to give up one's illusions, so I continued to vote NDP for many years. But it seems my initial facile equation was just an example of the American tendency to simplify what is foreign by clumsily superimposing hometown schemas.

Politics doesn't particularly interest me, and it probably doesn't particularly interest any reader who has got this far either. So I'll try to keep this simple, brief, and, I hope, germane to the theme of this book.

Politics: Our Quirky System

Yank Question: You keep electing a *"Liberal"* government. You guys commies?

Canuck Answer: Nah, we're not even *really* liberal, alas, but we like to think we are. (And it should be noted that we, at time of writing, have temporarily elected a Conservative minority government, largely because the Liberals were too 'liberal' with funding their friends at public expense.)

'Liberal' is an interesting word that has many meanings and has undergone many shifts in connotation as it shows its passport and crosses international borders. Its most amazing transformation is when crossing the Peace Bridge into The States, where the word, unlike anywhere else in the world, has a negative connotation.

Canada has a multi-party system, which while nowhere near as multi and chaotic as those of France or Italy is still confusing to folks who talk about red and blue states, who are accustomed to dichotomizing political positions. Up here we haven't learned to keep things so simple, or at least not so simple as to think political views can be neatly sorted into two boxes. I'm no political pundit—as God, and everyone, knows!—so I'm not sure where to begin. Maybe a good starting point is to list our major and minor parties with an admittedly biased description of their political agendas.

The Liberals. Don't let the name fool you! But, of course, by current Yank standards they might even be called The Bolsheviks. Something I must explain right now is that 'liberal' is not a dirty word in Canada, or, for that matter, anywhere in the civilized world except for large portions of the U.S. of A.—but then I did say 'civilized', didn't I? Generally, Canucks value a liberal education and liberal values—which include such things as human rights, tolerance of diversity and equal opportunity. (Or at least we, or most of us, *claim* to value and respect these things.) The Liberal Party, however, is not deeply committed to socialist reform, nor do its members seem especially concerned with promoting the high ideals of philosophical liberalism. The party's liberalism seems to have more to do with being liberal with tax-payers' dollars. Being a Liberal has more to do with attitudes about a liberal fiscal policy than it does about philosophical liberal values.

The Conservatives. Again, we are talking more about fiscal policy than values. It is true that if you are a Yankee Republican you are more likely to find a soul mate at a convention of Conservatives than at a Liberal convention, but many Conservatives are anything but socially conservative and would find a Yankee Republican a very strange bedfellow indeed. In fact, in Canada, many people who vote for the Conservative Party refer to themselves as Red Tories—meaning they are fiscally conservative, yet are what Yankees would consider 'pinkos' when it comes to social issues. In summary, Canadians make a distinction between fiscal and social conservatism—something a bit foreign to Yanks. I should say, however, that this distinction has become a little less clear with the new Conservative Party, which was clumsily welded together from the older Progressive Conservative Party (note that adjective) and a more socially conservative party called The Reform Party. But of course, few politicians practice what they preach. The current Bush Republican administration (allegedly 'conservative') is spending money like there is no tomorrow—which there might not be if they continue with their current foreign policy! And our own Conservatives haven't been particularly conserving either when they've held the reins of power.

The New Democratic Party. This is allegedly 'the party of conscience'. This is the party that is supposedly really, deeply, liberal—and less concerned with fiscal matters and more concerned with higher ideals, social justice and the common man. It had its quite noble origins, and found its electoral base, in the working class and in the community of intellectual, socially-concerned radicals. It continues to find its major support from these two groups, but two groups which have become more and more really uncomfortable in each other's presence—leading to its decline in popularity. One of its major leaders in recent times was an outspoken homosexual who was not exactly your typical working-class union member's idea of the best spokesman for their concerns. He has disappeared from the political scene because of being caught stealing expensive jewellery and confessing to "kleptomania disorder". One can easily imagine how this played out in the post teamster-union meetings get-togethers at the local pubs! The concerns of the working class and the concerns of far-left intellectuals have come to have less and less in common. It is an unfortunate fact of our time that The Left, obsessed with political correctness, is almost as guilty of human rights abuses and infringement on freedom of expression as The Right—and has proven totally ineffectual in really improving the plight of the common man—and woman. Example: in terms of policy, when this opposition party actually won power in Ontario, it managed to alienate everyone with Draconian anti-union policies, social policies that did more to hurt the poor than help them, irresponsible spending of tax-payers dollars, and mismanagement that rivalled anything done by previous administrations with less 'noble' ideals. The NDP is no longer a major political force but nonetheless remains one of Canada's four major parties.

The Bloc Quebecois. The existence of this federal party is either a demonstration of noble Canadian tolerance and unflinching commitment to democratic ideals—or proof positive that our system of government is based on a chapter that was excised, for being *too* absurd, from Lewis Carroll's *Alice In Wonderland*. The Bloc is a separatist party whose avowed goal is to dismantle Canada. (And this is currently the major opposition party federally!) The Provincial Government of Quebec has for many decades been talking about seceding from Canada, and we have even held federally sanctioned referenda that could have resulted in Quebec separating. Many Quebecers, with some justification, maintain they are a "distinct society"; i.e., a culture so different from the rest of English Canada that they should be a separate nation. Now Yanks (who are notoriously weak in geography) please note that Quebec is not on the outskirts of Canada, but embedded between Ontario and all the East Coast provinces, so such Quebec 'sovereignty' would mean a Quebec nation surrounded by Anglophone Canada. The fundamental absurdity of this arrangement is worth a book (and there are a few), but the point here is that this party is a *federal* party represented in our Parliament! Challenge your imagination: imagine that in The States there was a third party, a Confederacy Party, represented in Congress as the major opposition party, whose central political platform was the secession of all the States south of certain latitude, except (to improve the analogy) Florida! Oh, I cannot go on about this. Canadian politics is as surreal as Yank politics is sleazy.

Others—yes others!
And Canada also has a Green Party, a Communist Party (Yanks should exercise their imagination again and imagine the Communist Party Member from Kansas debating in Congress with the Republican from New York), and a Social Credit Party (and their policies are so flakey as to challenge a satirist, but they have occasionally wielded power in flakey B.C.). We also have members of Parliament who are 'Independents'. None of these currently have any federal seats, but they do sometimes affect the balance of power at provincial levels.

Federal versus Provincial Rights and Powers.
I should say something about this, and its parallels in the ongoing battle between States' rights and Federal rights. Both countries have since their inception been engaged in an internal power struggle between the pig-headed parts and the control-freak whole. The Yanks, typically, turned it into a full blown civil war at one point. The only time Canucks almost came to blows was when fringe radical Quebec separatists tried their hands at bombings and kidnapping in 1970 and Trudeau, the prime minister at the time, briefly invoked The War Measures Act—effectively setting up martial law. Unlike The States where The Civil War resulted in the death of over 120,000 people, the October Crisis death toll was less than thirty. What is interesting from a philosophical perspective, and this applies to both countries, is whether the provincial/state faction or the federalists are the good guys. But this is a question outside of the purview of this book, or my competence to answer, but it is worth noting that just as the federal government was eventually responsible for desegregation in The States, in Canada it is the federal government that installed our version of the Bill Of Rights—albeit with a bizarre "opt-out" clause for the provinces. But that's another (typically Canadian) story.

Update

This an update that is seriously required—and is very depressing to write. Canada has fallen from the high moral ground it once held internationally and now lies in ruins at the bottom of the ethical mountain. Canucks traveling abroad no longer attach a Canadian flag pin to their jackets or backpacks to be sure they aren't confused with Yanks, who aren't exactly welcome tourists (except for their money). And I can't be so smug in commenting to my in-laws (who all reside south of the border) about the latest, newsworthy example of Yank politics and international immorality.

This is the result of the new Conservative party, which had really become conservative in the worst possible meaning of the word, gaining majority rule. And because of their leader, Stephen Harper, being a dangerous (and successful) control freak. (Meanwhile, the Americans elected a smart, ethical man who was, astoundingly, of the 'wrong' skin colour!)

It doesn't say much for Canuck intelligence that Harper was elected, although those who would deny this solid empirical evidence of my over-estimation of my fellow citizens' sense and decency do have excuses for these election results. The two major non-conservative parties split the vote—which couldn't happen in the dichotomized U.S—and there also was some evidence of voting irregularities and some dirty tricks pulled by the Conservative party. I wish these excuses were adequate.

I'm a non-partisan kind of guy, and I'm not going to get on a political soapbox to rant about Harper's shrewd and evil machinations clearly focused on supporting big business, while happily trashing human rights, gagging scientists, polluting the environment, and working at undoing all the characteristics that had made Canada such a great country and so admired worldwide.

Suffice it say—and sorry to say—any Republicans visiting here won't feel quite so uncomfortable as they would have before our regime change.

Commies: Why Canucks Are Such Pinkos

Yank Question: So you have this socialized medicine and other Marxist stuff, and you folks even mix with dem Cubans—even buying and smoking their cigars. How come you're so pinko, when good old fashioned free enterprise gave you all the good stuff you have?

Canuck Answer: We're sluts, easy going opportunists. And Cuban cigars are *so* good. And if the number of signs offering them for sale in border towns such as Niagara Falls is any indicator, they're obviously popular with Yank tourists.

Well make no mistake; Castro *is* a nasty bit of business, probably guilty of almost as many human rights abuses as the current president of the United States—although I can't be absolutely sure he is up to that standard. I would like to believe that all communists—along with Hitler and all his Nazi buddies, all religious and political terrorists, all the Idi Amins and Papa Docs and Osama bin Ladens of the world, and certain American presidents—eventually end up down in Dante's Ninth Circle Of Hell—in a frozen lake with nothing to do but suffer excruciating pain and swap stories, between screams of agony, about their evil deeds. And I suspect most of my fellow Canucks (and most Americans) would share this view.

Canadians have as little use for totalitarianism (including communism as it has been implemented in the 20th Century) as do the alleged and self-appointed defenders of the free world to our south—in fact, I would venture to say even less use. However we do not, most of us, see concern with helping the disadvantaged as a threat to democracy. Only the ill-educated confuse socialism—yea, even liberalism—with communism. Most Canadians, much as they bitch about the *implementation* of their public health care system, do believe that every citizen should be supplied with government funded health care. It is just one of those things one forms a federal government to supply—like roads and bridges, defence against barbarian invaders, a police force to protect one from crazed criminals, legal protection of basic human rights, and National Holidays where everyone can get drunk and feel patriotic. Why else would the average Joe cough up at tax time every year almost half of his hard-earned roubles to the care of a bunch of sleazy politicians who are as capable of fairly distributing the monies they are entrusted with as they are capable of resisting the temptation to dip into the honey pot. The United States government is virtually alone in the civilized world in not guaranteeing primary health care to its citizens—and in viewing this as a slippery slope down to communism!

Yanks have to realize that their naïve world view of politics isn't shared by the citizens of other countries—not even Canadians, who *do*, alas, share a disturbing number of other prejudices. Canadians do not have the "us versus them", the "you're with us or against us" mentality that is so typical of an imperial power. We're more like the smallish kid in the playground who just wants to get along with everybody so nobody steals his lunch—which may explain why we're so embarrassed (albeit secretly pleased) when one of us lets slip a comment about the schoolyard bully, such as when one of our federal politicians got taped by a reporter referring to G.W. Bush as a "moron".

It also explains why we are willing to also be so discreetly buddy-buddy with the cigar smoking kid we all know is a tin-pot dictator kept in line by being bullied by a bigger bully. (I should say formerly cigar-smoking. He gave up the habit, and—surprise, surprise—is now enforcing strict no-smoking laws in nicotinic Cuba.)

Update

The obvious update to this is a correction to the references to the President of The United States. Americans impressed the world by electing Barack Obama. (Bush has retired to his ranch where he drifts into contented senility dabbing paint on canvas.) And Obama makes my comments about American healthcare out-dated. Mind you, the Republicans used their well-funded propaganda machine to continue to convince the naïve public it was a commie plot. Nevertheless, Obama still managed to pass over all the hurdles to implementation. While it isn't health care as fully governmentally funded as elsewhere in the civilized world, it does something to protect people from financial ruin when their health fails.

Terrorists: Why Canucks Are Not Paranoid

Yank Question: How come you don't do more to protect *us* from terrorists who are everywhere waiting to undermine the American Ideal of Freedom?

Canuck Answer: The 'American' Ideal of Freedom? Gimme a break! And although we know even paranoiacs have real enemies, we're not (at least not quite) as paranoid as Yanks. We do more than our share to combat real enemies. Yanks shouldn't blame their friends and neighbours for the actions of those that hate, alas only too often justifiably, America.

I don't mean to get serious. (Every time I do it ruins my digestion.) But a little righteous indignation, perhaps residual from my early years down below, seems in order here. When the twin towers were destroyed, Canadians (even those who generally harboured less than warm feelings toward Americans) bought decals to stick on their home and car windows that displayed the Canadian and American flags in virtual coitus with sayings expressing the idea that Canada is behind you one hundred percent and shares your pain.

Nothing in recent time did more to mend the rifts between the two countries than this horrible event. It was as if a marriage on the rocks was redeemed by one spouse's tragedy and the other's responsive compassion. Of course things have changed dramatically since 2001, largely thanks to G.W. Bush and his handlers who squandered this goodwill within months. It's as if you went to the funeral of a friend's spouse to express your condolences, and your friend accused you of somehow being complicit in the person's demise.

For example, The White House, whose own negligence and lack of vigilance is now well documented, took only a few days to blame Canada for being a portal of entry for terrorists. Subsequent intelligence shows this to be total nonsense, but more importantly the logic of this is comical. Let's work through the syllogism. Canada is too easy going in allowing 'aliens' in. Therefore, when the United States lets these dangerous enemies of America through its borders, it's not because *they* weren't vigilant at their own borders. Nah, it's because their neighbour let them get to that border via Canada. Huh? Duh?

And then later when Canada (along with most of the other democratic nations in the world) didn't just join in as allies in The United States' egregious war of aggression against Iraq, we were promptly tossed into that category of "those not with us, ergo enemies of us". If Canadian Bacon were as popular as French Fries, I'm sure Congress would officially have renamed it "Bush Bacon". (Incidentally, Canadians don't actually call it Canadian Bacon; they refer to it as "Back Bacon".)

But to return to my central point. What the average American needs to understand about Canada is that we do not have full-blown psychotic paranoia. The DSM-IV (the official diagnostic manual/bible for mental illness) differentiates between paranoid schizophrenia and the personality disorder (neurotic, as opposed to psychotic, disorder) called paranoid personality type. Well that is an apt description of the difference between Yank and Canuck mental dysfunction. It is said that neurotics build castles in the sky, and psychotics live in them. Canada has never had anything approaching McCarthyism, but this is not to say we don't have irrational fears. The lefties here fear that if someone can actually speed up medical care by resorting to private care at their own expense, this will somehow totally undermine the public medical care system and the poor will be left bleeding to death on the streets of Toronto. The rightists fear that if the government throws a few dollars to starving artists through our federal Canada Council of the Arts program, the country will go bankrupt from doling out below subsistent-level financial support to a few of those guys and gals who write incomprehensible poems and fling paint at canvas—and, furthermore, typically have nothing good, grateful and obsequious to say about the government. But these paranoid delusions do not lead to witch hunts like those initiated by McCarthy—or Johnson and Nixon during the Vietnam debacle.

While it *may* be that Americans actually have more guaranteed freedoms *on paper* (that paper being written 200 years ago by men who are now no doubt spinning in their graves as fast as the current politicos are 'spinning' the news), Canadians are in reality freer, less subject to governmental meddling in their lives and far less likely to suffer abuse at the hands of those in power suffering from paranoid dementia. And this has never been truer than now.

Update

If anything, Yanks have become more paranoid, and most Canucks still don't share this disorder. It has to be said, however, that our current government is especially complicit in infringing on the right to privacy, justifying it by the lame excuse of being necessary for protecting "national security". Such abuses by the NSA are constantly making the news, thanks to brave whistleblowers like Snowden. But even most Canadians probably have never heard of CSEC (Communication Security Establishment Canada), our collaborator with the NSA—and their loyal servant. And it isn't some insignificant branch office. The current government is funding new headquarters for CSEC in Ottawa costing close to a billion dollars.

So any American visiting Canada shouldn't expect to be out of sight of Big Brother's eye. In fact they may be watched more closely, because the NSA doesn't trust anyone who crosses the border.

Anti-Americanism: Why Canucks Don't Love Their Neighbours

Yank Question: Someone told me *Americans have something that neither Mexicans nor Canadians have*, but they didn't agree with any of my answers. They even insisted 'freedom' wasn't correct! So what's the right answer?

Canuck Answer: Good neighbours!

Sorry! It's another standard Canuck joke, although I think the original version was: "What do Swedes have that neither Norwegians nor Finns have?"

A joke, yes. But let me be blunt. The joke is no joke. And it is just one of many jokes Canucks love to tell about their southern neighbours. The brutal truth that I'm sure will surprise only too many Americans—although it shouldn't—is that they are not seen by the rest of the world as beacons of liberty and justice for all, as saviours of the world, as, even, particularly nice people. I think many of the people of Western Europe and Canada tend to view The Land Of The Free as being populated by—and run by—dangerous, self-deluded yokels. They are usually too tactful (and fearful) to be open about this opinion, although one of our politicians, as previously mentioned, was caught on tape with an offhand remark about George W. Bush being a "moron". I suspect this is a widely held opinion but one that, nevertheless, it is most undiplomatic to express. (This remark, unlike most of the utterances of our politicians, received considerable coverage below the border.)

I am *not* suggesting that it is fair, this evaluation of our Southern neighbours as being a bit—what would be diplomatic?—less than sophisticated, a bit educationally challenged. But neither do I want to be put in the difficult position of trying to defend my Fatherland from such an evaluation. *That* would be far too formidable a task.

The civilized world's ambivalence toward The States is astounding. Yankee ingenuity and bad taste (including bad tasting food) is widely admired and emulated, proving that Yanks don't have a monopoly on bad judgement. The rest of the world and The U. S. of A: Talk about a love/hate relationship! The United States of America is the home of some of the greatest minds—the finest artists, writers, musicians, scholars and scientists in the world. Yet its government has been, at least since the founding fathers, largely run by dolts elected by dolts. Alexis de Tocqueville realized the dangers of this experiment in egalitarian democracy two centuries ago.

And the rest of the world only knows about America from their experience with Yankee cultural imperialism, an appalling foreign policy based on self-righteous self-importance, and tourists—the notorious "Ugly Americans". (Ambrose Bierce once remarked that "To be a Frenchman abroad is to be miserable; to be an American abroad is to make others miserable.") A reasonable number of Canadians know Americans on another level: they have traveled south of the border and dealt with them in their own lairs. (Canadians venture south far more than Americans venture north.)

Most of my friends here have daringly traveled south into Yank territory. However, since Bush and his Home Security Gestapo have made such ventures a very unpleasant experience, more than a few of these friends of mine swear that they'll never cross that border again. One acquaintance, a professional psychologist, who regularly ran educational seminars in Vermont and New York simply refuses to offer them anymore after his repeated harassment at the border by semi-literates became too much to tolerate. Another friend, attending a conference on kids' educational toys, was so verbally abused at the NYC airport custom clearance that he swears he'll never set foot in The States again. This is sad, for most Canadians who have traveled in The States come home talking more about the friendliness of Americans than their less admirable traits. Oh, they also come home with tales of the appalling poverty and the dangerous neighbourhoods only a few city blocks from their five star hotels. But still Canadians, so naturally reserved, are quite impressed by Yankee casual friendliness. (This sort of casual friendliness does occur in Canada as well—primarily on the east coast, but that is for a later chapter.)

Now I know this is going to be hard to believe, given what I've already written, but Canadians don't really hate Americans. Americans, remember, being a nation of paranoid schizophrenics, manifest all the associated symptoms including delusions of grandeur and delusion of persecution. One of my Yank in-laws is always complaining about my wife's alleged "Yank bashing"—simply because she occasionally forwards new items from foreign news sources that report things, not reported in the mainstream American press, which do not cast American foreign policy in a favourable light.

So Americans should, in attempting to understand Canada's relationship with them, remember that being an American, despite what they might have been taught in school, does not automatically inspire undying love in all those who aren't Yanks. By various international criteria it never ranks as the best country to live in. Nevertheless, Canadians, like many people around the civilized world (at least that small part of the civilized world that hasn't been meddled with by the imperialists in the White House), admire and respect much about Americans including their accomplishments (not in terms of social justice, but in terms of the arts and sciences), their openness (even if it sometimes is comically naïve or, worse, rude), their relative success with building a country on revolutionary principles (hey, the French sure botched it a lot more before getting it right), and their collective personality (*sans* their paranoia and delusions of grandeur).

So advice to Yanks: Canadians aren't likely to hug you and offer you their daughters in marriage. But they—honest to God—don't hate you either and won't offer you poisoned beer. Most Canucks, I dare to generalize, would say: Yanks are nice people to have visit, and spend their Yankee bucks, but they wouldn't want most of them to live *here*.

I'm pleased to say they've made an exception in a few cases—such as mine.

Update

I think all of this is still very much the same, although the dislike of Americans in other countries has definitely escalated, and they re probably unabashedly hated even more than in the past. Even the Europeans are having a hard time remaining reasonably cordial, thanks to NSA snooping.

But most Canadians still welcome American visitors. And retired Canucks often escape to the south for a few months of our inclement winters. (They're called "Snowbirds", and their flocks often migrate to Florida for the winter.)

The usual impression I get from my fellow citizens returning from any time in The States is that it's a nice place to visit, but they wouldn't want to live there. I certainly feel that way.

Artsy and Entertaining—Well Sometimes

So what is 'Canuck Cultural Life' like? If one watches travel shows like *Lonely Planet/Pilot Guides,* one knows that travel journalists always try to find something unique and bizarre about a country's 'arts and entertainment scene' on which to report: A little throat singing, a bizarre Greek folk wedding dance where men demonstrate that white guys can't dance, or the sacrifice of a virgin at the mouth of volcano—anything a bit different from half-time at the Super Bowl or an MCTV music video. When their assignment is Canada, their creative ingenuity is really challenged. What can they possibly show to an American audience that is uniquely Canadian—*and* interesting? An Inuit party game played in an Igloo that involves seal skins and rubbing noses—or, in the X-rated version, swapping wives?

Well the sad truth is that Canadian culture (*culture* in the sense of the arts, not in the anthropological sense of ethnic eccentricities) bears far too close a resemblance to what passes for culture in The United States to be of particular interest except to those who look really closely. Canuck Culture is in fact so similar to Yank stuff as to 'pass' with most near-sighted Yanks—who almost always think our artists are American, not Canadian. (Being American is the default assumption, isn't it?) Of course Canadians, with their patriotic obsessions fuelled by a deep inferiority complex, make a big deal about reclaiming their native sons and daughters as icons of Kanadian Kulture.

There is no question that Canadian artists have a distinctive voice, but it is just one voice in the chorus of the Western Art tradition—and it sings in the same vocal range as their southern neighbours. Art in all its various 20th and 21st century manifestations is mostly orchestrated by Yanks. Who cares if the virtuoso first violinist is Bulgarian or Canadian—except the Bulgarians or Canadians?

For better or worse, The United States is the gold—or some would say fool's gold—standard for contemporary art and culture.

So for a Yank, getting a handle on Canadian culture only involves recognizing relatively fine distinctions in our approach to the arts. I like to think that we raise the standard, raise the bar, and while standing on the shoulders of our Yank—and sometimes British and French—predecessors, do really create art worthy of international recognition.

Cultural Protectionism: No Unguarded Borders For Culture

Yank Question: Why do Canadian radio stations play so many Joni Mitchell songs?

Canuck Answer: I wish it was just because she is *really* good and really important (which she is), but it's actually because she's a Canuck. Well, sort of. It doesn't matter to the CRTC that she's lived in the States since 1966. She was born in Fort McLeod, Alberta, and that redeems her.

Supplementary Yank Question: What the hell is the CRTC?

Canuck Answer: It's an acronym for **C**anuck **R**adio-**T**V and **T**elecom **C**ontrol-Freaks: a paternalistic, governmental organization putatively mandated to protect Canadian 'culture', which they do by censorship, by silly rules about the minimum percentage of Canadian content a radio station is required to air to remain licensed.

If you check out their website you are greeted with this message: "Welcome to the site of the Canadian Radio-television and Telecommunications Commission (CRTC). The CRTC is an independent agency responsible for regulating Canada's broadcasting and telecommunications systems. We report to Parliament through the Minister of Canadian Heritage." Up here, we're big on regulatory agencies to protect us from evil influences. (And I offer my apologies on their behalf for the implication that Yank Culture is an evil influence.)

Now far be it from me to deny that the trash that litters Yankee airways is evil—or, well, at least aurally toxic, but the libertarian Yank part of me balks at the idea that if I freely choose to poison the auditory cortex of my brain with Yahoo Yank Yak radio or Rabid Rap Riffs, I should be prevented from doing so by those who know better what is good for me. Well, not even prevented exactly—rather force-fed a percentage of Canuck stuff as a putative antidote. Aside from the obvious offensiveness of such paternalistic *hubris*, the fact is that the antidote served up is not even usually such good medicine as Joni Mitchell. Celine Dion and similar artificial sweeteners contaminate the concoction.

The CRTC website is a nightmare to navigate, as is to be expected of any governmental bureaucracy's website, so my patience is too limited to find out the exact percentage of Canadian content currently demanded of a radio or TV station—or the Kafkaesque rules defining what is "Canadian content". But the exact numbers don't matter: what matters is the underlying philosophy made (stupid) law.

.

That Americans are cultural imperialists is indisputable. (Why should imperialists in every other domain neglect culture?) But my adopted country embarrasses me with its fatuous and futile response to this. Even as pathologically ethnocentric and xenophobic as Yanks are, I'm sure they'd never pass legislation to restrict the number of tunes by "aliens" (as they designate anyone from another country in their immigration laws) that can be played on their radio stations. If memory serves, the so-called musical "British Invasion" spearheaded by The Beatles did not lead to Congress limiting the number of hits by the Fab Four that could be played on any radio station in any 24 hour period.

.

Now of course the justification for the CRTC and the various other forms of cultural protectionism practiced up here is allegedly noble and preached from high moral ground. We need to build high levees to prevent us from being swamped by the toxic waters lapping at the 49th parallel. We care about our artists, and have to protect them from unfair competition. Gimme a break. Yeah, right. If we really cared about our artists, we wouldn't be cutting federal and provincial grants to artists and publishers and cultural organizations every year since the glory days of spendthrift Prime Minister Trudeau. Oh, but governmental subsidizing of cultural endeavours is a violation of free trade! Oh then, of course restricting importation of Yank culture isn't? This whole issue of protectionism, alleged free trade, subsidies, import and export restrictions, and the rest of the whole political enchilada is too complex an issue for this small book—and my small brain.

.

What is relevant here is understanding Canadian reactions, official and in the streets, to the flood of American so-called 'culture' into our land.

.

Most Canucks love it. They gulp down the toxic waters as fast as they breach our flimsy governmental levees and fill the common trough. We listen to American pop music. We watch Hollywood movies. We read the books on the New York Times bestseller list. At least in the most popular of the popular domains—movies and pop music—the huge and powerful American industries just treat Canada as a fifty-first state.

.

Canadians developed a distinctively Canadian style at least a hundred years later than the Americans did. Americans had to free themselves from the British aesthetic, and they did so the same way they freed themselves from British rule: violently and drastically. Yanks still venerate their early artistic revolutionaries. Consider, for example, how drastically different are writers such as Walt Whitman, Emily Dickinson, Edgar Allan Poe from the British writers of the time. Or in music, consider the invention of a totally new art form: jazz. Well, Canadians took a different, more typically Canadian path. Remember the hackneyed comparison of revolution to evolution as describing respectively Yank versus Canuck approaches to change. Initially Canada also had to separate itself from the motherland of England, but it did so less radically, more gradually. And by then it had a new challenge: distinguishing itself from America. This is much harder and taking longer—and is less dramatic.

But any reasonable investigation of this topic requires making distinctions between 'high culture' and 'pop culture'. And, also, there are major differences in the different arts, so let me get a little more specific.

Update

What to add? Well, the major change is that cultural isolationism is being totally undermined by the Internet offering easy access to anything imaginable. The CRTC can regulate Canadian content on radio and TV to their bureaucratic heart's content, but who the hell listens to radio or watches TV anymore? We access our arts digitally. The Internet is a multicultural smorgasbord. And I think one of the effects of this is less concern in Canada, and everywhere else for that matter, about where the artist was born or if the style could be tagged as being distinctively associated with one place.

Literature: Canucks Can Read—And Really Do

Yank Question: How come Canucks talk so funny?

Canuck Answer: They know how to read, and sometimes (alas not often enough) it affects their speech. Or does that question refer to our unusual punctuation mark: "eh?"

I used to edit and publish a small literary magazine. Literary magazines, like poetry books, have a very limited (downright miniscule) audience in North America. One interesting statistic I came across back then in the early seventies was that the average print-run of a volume of poetry or a literary magazine published in The States was about 1,000. In Canada it was—about 1,000. Now given that The United States has 10 times the population of Canada, this indicates something.

I teach statistics, so I'm only too aware of how they can be misleading, but let me tread where only fools dare and cite a few numbers—largely letting them speak for themselves.

United States population: 298,444,215
United Kingdom population: 60,609,153
Canada population: 33,098,932

So England et al has approximately one-fifth the population of The States, and Canada has slightly more than one-tenth of the population of The States.

I did a quick internet search and found data from the British Council's The Publisher Association: Global Publishing Information database about the number of new books published in 1996 (the most recent year with data for all three countries available). Here are these data.

United States: 58,465 new titles released
United Kingdom: 102,102 new titles released
Canada: 18,573 new titles released

Get out your calculator. If these data are to be believed the U.K. publishes almost twice as many books per year as the United States even though they have only one-fifth the population! And Canada? We publish more than three times the number of books *per capita* than the U.S., albeit still less than half as many *per capita* as the U.K.

I don't necessarily trust the precision of these statistics, but even if the standard error of measurement is large, the pattern certainly confirms my subjective impressions. The Brits read a lot. The Canucks read less then the Brits, but still read far, far more than the Yanks. I'm well aware that number of books published may not be perfectly correlated with number of books read, but one could look at any number of different measures, and I'm quite sure that the same pattern would emerge. I leave it to the empirically minded reader to check out literacy statistics, academic achievement test scores, or any other appropriate indicator for the three countries, but I'd bet big money on the pattern being the same no matter which indicator is chosen.

This is also reflected in the quality of the television news broadcasts. Since most Canadian homes have cable or satellite reception, we have the opportunity to compare U.S. news with our several Canadian stations including CBC (the Canadian Broadcasting Corporation) as well as the BBC (British Broadcasting Corporation). Well, let's call a spade a spade here. Major network stations such ABC or NBC are slightly less appalling than CNN and downright highbrow compared to Fox, but the entire aforementioned are embarrassingly crass, simple-minded and childish compared to our CBC—which, alas, in turn seems just barely literate compared to the professionalism of the BBC.

But all this shouldn't be interpreted as suggesting that most Canucks speak the Queen's English even when quaffing beer at the local 'hotel'—with the only difference being a tendency to toss an "eh?" at the end of sentences. Nor is it to imply Canucks are all bookworms whose idea of a wild night on the town is attending a poetry reading or book signing. It's just that compared to what most Americans have experienced in the security (they are so anxious to protect) of their homeland, Canadians may seem just a bit more interested and knowledgeable about books and ideas. Our CBC radio has a talk-radio call-in show that a friend of mine says attracts "every asshole with a quarter or a cell-phone" and where the level of discourse (while hardly elevated) is, when compared to Yank talk-radio shows, equivalent to the difference between a bar-fight and an Oxford University debate.

Of course, Canada has its share of Yahoos and illiterates—and these folk have more in common with each other, no matter what country they hale from, than do any other social group on the planet. They, however, are not reading this book. What I have had to say applies, as far as any of my generalizations can apply, to the average middle-class guy or gal.

Update

Just like so many other things, the digital revolution has affected readers—and writers' publishers. So the statistics cited can no longer be trusted. More people are reading books on their Kindles and iPads, and more books are being published in digital format. And the evidence seems to indicate that one unexpected result of this is more, not fewer, people reading. And writing with a relatively small interested audience (e.g., poetry) is reaching more people, because of the decrease in expense for publishing digitally.

I still think, or at least like to believe, that the average Yank still doesn't read as much as the Canuck.

Music: We Gave Ya Our Best

Yank Question: Is it really legal to share music up there—oh, and by the way, what's Canadian music?

Canuck Answer: That's two questions. But to answer the first: yes more or less—as explained in an earlier chapter. And to answer the second: it's a small but respectable percentage of the best stuff you probably thought was American music.

Here is a short list. Many of these names are surely familiar; and these singers, songwriters, performers, bands, and composers, representing the whole gamut of musical genres, from classical through jazz and folk to pop, all have Canuck pedigrees: Bryan Adams, Paul Anka, April Wine, Jann Arden, The Arrogant Worms, Bachman-Turner-Overdrive, Barenaked Ladies, Jane Bunnett, Robert Charlebois, Bruce Cockburn, Leonard Cohen, Holly Cole, The Cowboy Junkies, The Crash Test Dummies, Maynard Ferguson, Ferron, Glenn Gould, The Guess Who, Corey Hart, Jeff Healey, Colin James, Oliver Jones, Dianne Krall, Chantal Kreviazuk, k.d. lang, Daniel Lanois, Gordon Lightfoot, Guy Lombardo, Kate & Anna McGarrigle, Ashley MacIsaac, Loreena McKennitt, Sarah McLachlan, Joni Mitchell, Alanis Morissette, Anne Murray, Jon Kimura Parker, Oscar Peterson, Luc Plamondon, The Rheostats, Robbie Robertson, Garnet Rogers, Stan Rogers, Rough Trade, Rush, Buffy Sainte-Marie, Paul Shaffer, Jane Siberry, Skinny Puppy, Hank Snow, Teresa Stratas, The Tea Party, Shania Twain, Steppenwolf, The Tragically Hip, Gino Vannelli, Roch Voisine, Rufus Wainwright, Neil Young.

Differences in musical tastes easily lead to bar fights, and this list contains *some* artists that could make even mild-mannered me aggressive toward anyone denying that they are duds, an aural blight on the musical landscape. (I won't mention names such as Celine or Bryan.) But it also contains many more folk who, were I to get puffed up with Canuck nationalism, I'd be proud to call my brethren.

But the point here is that unlike the British Invasion, when Britishness was way cool and exotic (and so no one thought The Beatles were American), Canadian musicians and performers are usually only recognized as being Canadian by Canadians. This irks a lot of Canucks, who feel credit should be given where credit is due. But of course the reason for this isn't *only* Yankocentricism and ignorance; it is also because there really aren't two distinct musical cultures in North America—just one, which (like it or not Canucks!) is predominately an American genre. Our best artists may have added their particular spices to the stew and extended its range of flavours, but its base stock is still American.

.

Examples abound. Oscar Peterson is indisputably one of the all time jazz greats, and his home town of Montreal rivals or surpasses any Yank city as a jazz centre. Its annual summer jazz festival is considered by more than a few aficionados to be one of *the* greatest annual jazz festivals in the world. But the indisputable fact is that jazz is a Yank invention. Yes, Peterson wrote a wonderful composition call *The Canadian Suite*, but ultimately there is nothing in his music that ear-marks it as "Canadian Jazz". (He also wrote a brilliant jazz rendition of *West Side Story* music, which is as American a film and soundtrack as one can conceive.)

.

Or consider Robbie Robertson. What could more typify late sixties American musical culture than The Band? And what Yank has drawn a musical portrait of New Orleans to compare with his conceptual album *Storyville*? Robertson's father was Jewish but his mother was Mohawk, and he spent part of his youth on the Six Nations Reserve in Ontario. In 1960 he met the famous and influential Ronnie Hawkins, who although born in Arkansas, many Canadians would claim as their native son, because he left The States to "bring rock and roll to Canada"— something he did with a passion. He bought a farm in Mississauga, Ontario, (now a suburb of Toronto) and then he, his band "The Hawks", and his many protégés changed the Canadian musical landscape forever. He has played for every Canadian Prime Minister since John Diefenbaker, our PM in the late fifties and early sixties. Ronnie and Robbie in many ways epitomize the fundamentally hybrid (or mongrel, if you like) nature of North American music and Canada's contribution to it: respectively, the American born musician reshaping the Canadian musical landscape and the Canadian born musician so defining the American musical landscape.

.

Before I step out of my role as music critic (for which I will openly admit I am ill-qualified), I just have to say something about Daniel Lanois, for he seems to me the most distinctively Canadian in the list—and is so because he epitomizes a cosmopolitanism that is paradoxically Canadian, yet he is 'provincial'. (The word *provincial* has come to mean "limited in perspective; narrow and self-centered; unsophisticated". Canada is made up of provinces. But in reality, the individual states are far more provincial in that sense of the word.) Lanois was born in Hull Quebec in 1951 to musical French-Canadian parents, but in 1963 moved to Canada's very Anglo steel-town—Hamilton, Ontario. *Rolling Stone* magazine called him "the most important record producer to emerge in the Eighties." For a musician to have an album produced by Lanois is roughly equivalent to a visual artist being selected to have a retrospective exhibition installed at the MET. Those so honoured include Brian Eno, Peter Gabriel, Bob Dylan, Wille Nelson, U2, Emmylou Harris, Robbie Robertson, and The Neville Brothers. But the reason I single him out as most archetypally Canadian is his own musicianship. His own albums brilliantly blend our so-called "two cultures". One only has to listen to the bilingual masterpiece "Jolie Louise" to understand. Anyone who doesn't have his heart ripped to pieces by this work has no soul—and probably shouldn't be permitted to breed.

Update

And so it still goes, although as mentioned earlier, one's nationality (however defined) is of less importance to people, even Canadians, than it once was. It doesn't matter so much that Justin Beiber was born in London, Ontario and raised in Stratford, Ontario—and I strongly suspect most self-respecting Canadians would like to keep that embarrassing fact a secret.

Film: It Ain't Hollywood But It Ain't Bergman Either

Yank Question: Is there such a thing as a Canadian movie? And how can I identify it?

Canuck Answer: We do make films—although not that many movies—and you can recognize one of our own by three things: 1) it just looks different, like it was made with an entry-level video camera; 2) it doesn't involve blowing up a lot of things; 3) it has characters that aren't two-dimensional.

Hollywood makes movies. Europeans make films. Canadians make videos. I don't mean that literally, but there is something about many of our films that just looks different—looks more like a video or a TV show than a film. If my son and I are flipping through the movie channels, we sometimes both exclaim simultaneously: "That's gotta be a Canadian film." And we're almost always right. I can't say exactly what it is, but many, or at least a fair number of, Canadian films just don't have that sheen or gloss or polish or whatever that one has come to expect of movies—and even of European films. Since most Canadian productions are made on a shoestring budget, maybe the processing is being sent out to Shopper's Drug Mart Photomart when they're running a sales special?

But, forgetting about this superficial distinction, and to return to the more substantive film versus movie distinction: the connotation of 'movie' is spectacle, popular entertainment; the connotation of 'film' is serious drama, high art. It may only be because the Canadian Film Industry is a cottage industry that can't afford to aim for movie status that our stuff bears more resemblance to the 'art films' of Europe than to typical Hollywood flashy fluff. It would be nice to think it has less to do with money and more to do with aesthetic sophistication, but I have no evidence of that.

Now I don't mean to imply that Canadian films are on par with Fellini, Bergman, or Truffaut. We have created a few masterpieces (more often than not originating in Quebec) that can compete in the big leagues, but if you browse critics' lists of the 100 greatest films of all time, you won't find any of ours that made the cut, while you will find many that originated in maligned Hollywood. So we may still be at the bottom of the league, but at least we're playing in the big leagues. Meanwhile, the American film industry plays in every league it can, and Hollywood's bad rep comes from all its bush leaguers. (I know it's unfair, for who would deny big league status to Welles or Kubrick or Scorsese?) But my point is that I can't imagine anything like *The Greatest Story Ever Told* or *Friday The 13th Part VIII: Jason Takes Manhattan* or *Independence Day* ever being created in Canada. To again switch metaphors, we Canucks more consistently aim higher, even if our guns are Saturday Night Specials and our aim often less than accurate.

Still we do hit the target occasionally. Film buffs will certainly recognize some of these names: Denys Arcand, James Cameron, David Cronenberg, Atom Egoyan, Norman Jewison, Claude Jutra, Allan King.

They will also recognize these Canuck filmic masterpieces (or, usually on the contrary, box-office successes): *Crash, C.R.A.Z.Y., Dead Ringers, Le Déclin de l'empire américain (The Decline of the American Empire), Exotica, Highway 61, Les Invasions Barbares (The Barbarian Invasions), Jésus de Montréal (Jesus of Montreal), Mambo Italiano, Margaret's Museum, Meatballs, Mon oncle Antoine, Porky's, Scanners, The Statement, Thirty Two Short Films About Glenn Gould, Videodrome, Whale Music.*

Still, if I had to find one word to describe our *average* film it would be two words: quirky and serious, yet funny. And sometimes pretentious, arty, badly edited, self-important, trite, poignant, silly, almost profound, weird. Oops, that is more than two words. Okay, how about un-American.

Update

One thing that has changed is the number of good (and bad) movies made *in* Canada, not necessarily *by* Canadians. It's much cheaper to film in Canada than The States (for various reasons), and Canada has good locations.

Our major cities (Toronto, Vancouver, and Montreal) can pass for any big American city—and there is less garbage to be picked up before beginning a shoot. Hollywood filmmakers know their audience and like to set their films in American locales. With a little 'make-up' Canadian cities can fool viewers. They are used in the same way Hollywood uses a body double for nude scenes that the high-priced star won't do. For example, "The Hulk" doesn't bulk up and turn green in the Big Apple, but actually in Toronto.

Oh, how typically Canadian, to contribute but remain unacknowledged!

Performing Arts: Scalping Tickets At The Reserve

Yank Question: What are 'performing arts"?

Canuck Answer: Maybe I'm wasting my time writing this book.

I'll keep this brief. We don't have Carnegie Hall. We don't have Radio City Music Hall. We don't have Broadway. We don't even have Off-Broadway. This may have something to do with us not having New York City itself and its ready access to a huge potential audience—even at the outrageous admission prices charged. NYC's population is over 8 million packed into 321 square miles. The total population of Canada is a mere 4 times that, and it is spread out over almost 4 *million* square miles, albeit most of our population has precipitated down to within a hundred miles of the U.S. border, clumping in cities.

Nevertheless, our larger cities do have major venues for the performing arts. Even the small Ontario towns of Stratford and Niagara On The Lake host internationally acclaimed theatre productions; i.e., The Shakespeare Festival and The Shaw Festival respectively, although neither limits its productions to works by these giants. And if you're in Toronto or Montreal or Vancouver or Winnipeg or Edmonton, you won't have any problem finding major concerts, ballets, operas or theatrical productions to attend. Of course, none of these cities offers the variety of a London, New York, or Paris, but if you're like me, and like most less-than-wealthy Yanks and Canucks, we can't afford to indulge in this sort of entertainment very often anyway. It's a special occasion sort of thing. Well, as such it can be found up here in the Northern cities just as easily as down in NYC—or Cleveland.

And as far as more modest performing arts go, even the smallest communities in Canada have active amateur theatre groups, pubs that feature traveling musical performances on weekends, and arts community centres that bring in touring performers of every stripe. This often means one can see a lot more up-close-and-personal—and at a smaller price— really incredible first-rate performers.

In fact, many star performers seem to like to play relatively small Canadian venues, perhaps because of nostalgia for their less-famous days or perhaps because Canuck club audiences are so respectfully enthusiastic. The Rolling Stones routinely do surprise warm-up concerts at a small club in Toronto. I heard Miles Davis at a small jazz club in Toronto just after he brought out his ground-breaking *Bitches Brew* album. I was close enough to see if he had a pimple on his nose—but for the fact he was doing his back-to-the-audience shtick. I heard B.B. King at an open air concert at Ontario Place, and was close enough to see the scratches on his beloved Lucille guitar. At same venue I had a drop of sweat fly off the brilliant and beautiful ballerina Karen Kain, and land on my cheek from my (free) front row seat. (I didn't wash my face for weeks.)

Canada ain't Hicksville.

Update

In general the arts scene has changed significantly since this was written, but the fundamental differences between Canada and The States has remained pretty much the same.

Canada's (Split) Personality

Canada is weird, and some of this weirdness is understandable given its history. I suppose there are cultures even more diametrically opposed than French and English, but certainly these two make very strange bedfellows. And in Canada they're still pulling the sheets off each other and complaining about each other hogging the bed. A bad marriage? I don't think that's fair. I think it was a marriage of *in*convenience that really hasn't worked out all that badly. French and English Canada are an old quarrelsome couple, but either would be devastated if their mate were to move on.

Schizophrenia is often confused with multiple-personality disorder—which is an entirely different form of mental illness. The 'schizo' in schizophrenia refers to dissociation of consciousness with unconsciousness. Well, Canada may indeed be a little schizoid, but I think multiple-personality disorder better fits the DSM-IV description. Psychiatric, and Hollywood pop-psych, poster child Eve allegedly had three faces, and Canada is traditionally considered just two-faced: Janus Canada, not Cerberus Canada! But that's only partially true. Canada's immigration policies have put the 'multiple' into multiple-personality disorder with a vengeance.

The U.S. has its 'melting pot' into which its immigrants are supposedly melted down into the homogenous pig iron called 'An American'. Canada, on the other hands, has been compared (by our eminent historian, John A Porter) to a fruitcake. All our immigrants are expected to keep their cultural identity, but keep it embedded in the sticky texture of the Canadian cake. "Multiculturalism" is a big buzz word here, and expressing any reservations about its sometimes crazed applications is equivalent to bad-mouthing motherhood or apple pie. Well, actually probably worse, since mothers' concerns don't get the same political attention that anyone who cries 'racism' gets.

But anyhow, on to an analysis of our personality disorders.

Two Cultures: Actually Three Plus N

Yank Question: Are most Canadians bilingual, and how did that happen?

Canuck Answer: Yes, most Canadians can speak both English *and* American. Some are even trilingual and can also speak French!

Okay, this is going to get complicated. We are a primitive people, but unlike the 19th century Khoikhoi, we do have an integer counting system that makes more distinctions than one, two, three, and many. But I'm going to use this system in accordance with the rule (apt for instructing Yanks) that one should keep it simple.

Canada is the mongrel offspring of three cultures: British, French, and American. One, two, three. We also have in recent years welcomed N (N=many) immigrants from all around the world. This complicates the equation beyond consideration here. For practical purposes, understanding the collective Canuck personality it is adequate to deal with the big three: Brits, Frogs, and Yanks.

John Robert Colombo (a *very* Canadian Canadian) once remarked that Canada could have enjoyed: English government, French culture, and American know-how. But instead it ended up with: English know-how, French government, and American culture. That is certainly one reasonable way to delineate our personality disorder.

Another comparison that comes to mind is Freudian. Let's assign the British influence to Freud's superego (that nagging, somewhat prissy voice of one's conscience), and then assign the id (that libido-crazed, screw-anybody in one's way, instant-gratification devil's whisper) to the Yanks—and finally call the French influence (and this is less convincing a parallel) the ego which manages to diplomatically resolve conflicts between the other two extremes.

But to most Canadians, the deeply ingrained American part of their personality is hardly noticed, and they remain obsessed with the infamous two cultures that are their historic heritage: French and English. Upper and Lower Canada. Quebec which was founded by the French and the rest of the country which was founded by the British.

(Both these cultures currently are so heavily influenced by their southern neighbours that I suspect a Londoner or Parisian visiting Toronto or Montreal, respectively, would probably detect more similarity to the U.S. in the local culture than to their homeland.)

So what about these two cultures defines my country? When I came here in my youth I was fond of propounding my theory as to why Canada was so much less ethnocentric, narcissistic, and all kinds of other egotistical things: it was because Canada had *two* cultures: the French and the English. We had two languages. We had two very different sets of cultural values. Yet we lived together harmoniously, and learned to appreciate that whatever cultural value-set we had inherited from our parents wasn't necessarily the gold standard. Yeah, right.

Unfortunately the two major treats in Canada's fruit cake are rarely close enough to blend flavours. Canada's Prime Minister, Pierre Trudeau, for the first decades of my residence here was an aristocratic Quebecer, an intellectual, a liberal, and an impassioned promoter of bilingualism. (The average Yank seemed to think he was a crazed hippie, pinko radical who wore sandals and went on holidays to Cuba where he smoked Cuban cigars with Fidel and hit on the young ladies. Oh yes, he was a bachelor as well!) Well, the Trudeaumania (as it was called), like Beatlemania, seemed to infect the younger generation and then eventually subsided when he alienated the Anglo Canadians by what they viewed as shoving French down their throats and alienated the Quebecois by his installation of martial law when a few crazed Quebec separatists lost their marbles. But that's another story—and a complicated one. (The great Canadian poet Irving Layton expressed his disillusionment with Trudeau's fall from liberal grace by the remark: "Canada has at last produced a political leader worthy of assassination." I, however, think Layton was being a bit harsh.)

But what is germane to this biased little primer is that visiting Yanks won't much notice that much French influence in English Canada, except for all the packages of anything they buy having everything written in both French and English. And, if in Quebec, the English will be in small print—even on storefronts in Anglo neighbourhoods. (It's the law. But that's another sad story.)

Update

The separatist movement has lost its momentum, which was largely supported by the young—who no longer are quite so young. Anglophone Canadians seem more tolerant of the French and their chauvinistic linguistic protectionism. And the French have, despite their fears, been infiltrated by Anglophone culture, albeit primarily American.

Quebec remains the distinct culture they have always claimed to be, but their culture also remains quite distinct from that of France. And both English *and* French Canadian culture have become even less distinct from American culture.

One obvious omission in the original discussion that I should address is the other truly distinct culture: that of the original Canadians. What to say about Native culture(s)? Certainly they might be considered separatists, for *all* the rest of Canada is populated by pushy immigrants who seem to want these original inhabitants to behave just act like another group of newcomers—and politely find a place in the Canuck fruitcake. I suppose that's slightly better than being thrown into the Yank melting pot. But it's still ridiculous.

Mores And Folkways: Deference Differences

Yank Question: How come Canadians are so *polite*?

Canuck Answer: And what the fuck do you mean by that, you asshole?! Just kidding! We're polite because of relativity theory. Compared to Americans, the Vandals were polite, the Visigoths downright obsequious.

We really aren't *that* polite. I mean, really, we don't have different pronouns to address each other formally or informally as do the Germans and the French. (Well, oops, I should say we Anglophone Canadians don't. Still, Francophone Canadians don't take this formal/informal distinction as seriously as those in France.) You'll be hard put to find anywhere in Canada where rigid rules of etiquette, such as those adhered to by upper class Brits, are normal. Nor are we like the Brits in that we don't, at the slightest provocation, queue up in orderly fashion like Emperor Penguins on their long march to their breeding ground. And when we belch after a good meal, as we may often do, we don't do so because it is considered good breeding and a compliment to the chef. We're just prone to gas from drinking too much beer.

An important distinction is in order here. There is *politeness*. And there is *courtesy*. Politeness refers to conforming to the social norms, the accepted etiquette of the time and place one finds oneself in. Courtesy refers to showing respect and consideration for those around you. Any given action can be both polite and courteous or it can be just one and not the other—or, of course, it can be neither. In many places it is not considered impolite to arrive late for an appointment, but nevertheless it *is* discourteous if one knows the other person is on a tight schedule and can't afford to be kept waiting. It may be impolite to use the wrong form of address to an elder or eat one's peas with one's knife or put on a seat belt in a taxi in Eastern Europe, or light a cigarette in a young Yuppie Canadian couple's home, or tell a guest in a Lithuanian home that he has to stand outside in the cold if he wants to smoke, or call one's waitress "sweetie", or call the waiter at MacDonald's "*garcon*", but it is only discourteous if one does so knowing it will cause offence.

Courtesy requires thoughtfulness and sincere consideration of other people. Politeness only—but essentially—requires knowledge of the rules of the social game as played in some particular place and time. Big diff.

I think Americans can expect Canadians to be a wee bit more *courteous* than they're accustomed to, but I may be giving us Canucks too much credit. (It's certainly not a position I'd want to defend to the death.) Nonetheless, I'm sure our reputation for being polite (at least compared to what the average Yank is accustomed to) *is* justified. However, it has more to do with just that: *politeness*—not courtesy. At least in English Canada, where residual British influence regarding manners still is of some significance, some reserve is considered polite. And, conversely, such lack of reserve, more common in our Southern neighbours, is oft times considered impolite, even barbaric. Although many Canadians, being more familiar with Yanks than vice versa, are simply inclined to view American tourists' often gauche behaviour as strangely charming, as nothing more than slightly inappropriate friendliness.

An exemplary anecdote. My family and I were on an outdoor patio in a restaurant on Place Jacques Cartier in the Old Port area of Montreal. Some boisterous American tourists arrived—half a dozen loud, loutish middle-aged men. They made lame, semi-literate—but not at all malicious—jokes about the French. One particularly—shall we say 'extroverted'—guy kept doing what I think he viewed as clever flirting with the waitress. He kept calling her "Sweetie" and asking silly questions about menu items (which were printed in plain English). What is interesting and instructive here is the reactions of the various spectators to this traveling circus of Yankee Yahoos.

My wife and I and my son (who was born in Canada and had lived in various European countries for eight years) were both amused and mildly appalled by what we viewed as stereotypically barbaric Yank Tourist behaviour. My daughter, also born in Canada, but who was at the time working on her Ph.D. at Brown in Rhode Island, and had made many friends there, was a bit defensive about our sniggering at this motley crew and the loudmouth who was harassing the waitress. "He's just being friendly," she insisted. I observed the other patrons, a mixture of Quebecers and tourists from English Canada, and I think the word that best describes their reaction would be: *bemusement*. And the waitress, a very attractive and self-possessed young woman and obviously a native Montrealer, probably a university student on a summer job, what was her reaction? Offended? Irritated? Unable to resist the urge to roll her eyes in amazement at such a lout? No, not at all. She was as gracious and charming in dealing with this group and this clown as she was with the elegantly dressed and dignified family conversing in French at the next table.

I think most Canadians actually like, even admire, their southern neighbours, at least in an individual vis-à-vis situation, for their forthrightness. This response, however, is probably framed within a condescending sense of superiority. Perhaps it's a bit like how straight-laced adults admire and envy little children's innocent expression of whatever is on their minds—yet still feel superior. Most Canadians have been too inculcated with quasi-British 'manners' (politeness and reserve) to behave in such an uninhibited fashion—even when on holidays in a foreign country. Only when individual American visitors behave discourteously, not merely impolitely, do the locals take offence. Canadians (being much more cosmopolitan than the average American) are accustomed to tourists carrying in their baggage very different and looser definitions of politeness. Besides, many Canucks rely on tourists, even the proverbial "Ugly American" ones, for their income. We are also a practical people.

In thinking about my reaction to the fellows in the Montreal restaurant in contrast to my reaction to waitresses in the southern states during a bike trip there, I realize that I'm too context dependent and my daughter was right. When a waitress (I never saw before in my life) in some small Louisiana town kept calling me "Honey", I didn't get my hackles up and reply: "I'm not your f'ing 'honey'!" Yet in Montreal I have to admit I kept wishing that waitress would tell her customer that she wasn't his f'ing "Sweetie". Oh well—just goes to show, remembering my Yank paternity, I'm a little embarrassed at the behaviour of my half-brothers.

In summary, more Canucks than Yanks have learned the lessons of please and thank you and have been taught not to be too 'forward'. But actually we are far less obsessed with politeness than most cultures, and probably are seen as only slightly less barbarous than Yanks when traveling abroad.

Update

Having visited The States numerous times since writing this, I can't say I feel that much has changed. Again I did notice how great the differences are from place to place. My daughter now lives in Boulder, Colorado, which is certainly an enclave of civilization. If the residents there were typical of everywhere south of the border, I'd have to say Yanks have learned some manners without losing their informal friendliness. But I know they have not.

Humour: Over Your Head And Below The Belt

Yank Question: What's with Canuck humour? I don't get it.

Canuck Answer: Actually you *do* get it a lot of the time, because we export more comedians than we do lumber. You just don't know they're from here. The rest of the time, it's just too subtle (or, to be kind, too culturally specific) for you to understand.

There is a clear difference between Yank and Canuck yuks. Humour is even harder to translate than poetry, because differences in humour are embedded in cultural—not just linguistic—differences. Up here we speak the same language as down below—more or less. (We pronounce *humour* the same as our Southern neighbours even if we insert that British 'u' in our spelling of the word.) But if you tell a Newfie joke—or worse still, a politically satirical joke—to a fella from Illinois, he is likely as not to look at you with the same blank stare that you'd get if you read him a bad translation of an Armenian joke about sheep.

Oh, not always, of course, for many of our comedic writers and performers have quite successfully exported their Northern brand of humour to The States for fame and fortune—and a green card. In fact, Canucks are embarrassingly proud of these turncoat comedians who have wooed American audiences.

So to be such a good, embarrassingly proud Canuck, here again is a short list of Northern Notables—some actors, some writers, some stand-ups, and many all three: Dan Aykroyd, John Candy, Jim Carrey, Thomas Chong of Cheech and Chong, Marie Dressler, David Foley, Tom Green, Don Harron, Phil Hartman, Stephen Leacock, Eugene Levy, Rich Little, Norm MacDonald, Howie Mandel, Andrea Martin, Lorne Michaels, Rich Moranis, Mike Myers, Catherine O'Hara, Mort Sahl, Mack Sennett, Martin Short, Frank Shuster and Johnny Wayne of Wayne and Shuster, Steve Smith, David Steinberg, Dave Thomas, Scott Thompson,

This list is largely based on a wonderful Canadaphile website in California (particle.physics.ucdavis.edu/Canadians), but it is by no means inclusive. It doesn't mention that Jack Warner of Warner Brothers, the company responsible for Bugs Bunny and all those very Looney Tunes, was also Canadian. Nor does it mention Michael J. Fox—an omission that wounds me deeply since he briefly attended school in the small city where I reside. Sigh.

Then there are the infamous MacKenzie Brothers (Bob and Doug) of *Strange Brew* fame, which Yanks will know are Canucks because their whole comedic shtick consists of acting out the most outrageous stereotypes of dim-witted, beer-guzzling Canuck hicks. I'm sure many a Yank knows about "eh" as a punctuation mark, "hoser" as Canuck Speak for loser, and "24" as meaning a case of brew because of these two very funny clowns.

And let us not forget that great Canadian: William Shatner. He even has a building at Montreal's McGill University named after him, as he was one of their alumni. (I think he actually graduated; I should look that up.) Not a comedian, you say?! Really? Go back and watch the original series Star Trek episodes again—or listen to his recent CD.

But those mentioned above are comics who 'made it' south of the border, and so comprise a somewhat biased sample. To get a proper perspective on Canadian humour one needs to watch Canadian TV and listen to Canadian radio, especially CBC; one needs to sample some of the home-grown stuff that has yet to be exported—and the reason it has yet to be exported may be that it, like a fine whine (pun intended), doesn't travel well. I don't know. Humour is not only very culturally specific; it is also very much a matter of personal taste.

I grew up in Chicago, watching sitcoms on the tube; and, in the movie theatre, so-called romantic comedies; and listening to, in the unhallowed halls of my high school, racist (and 'racy') jokes that would get one sued were one to repeat them now within earshot of one of our ever-vigilant, politically-correct vigilantes. I do remember laughing—at least I think I do—whether because Yank humour was funnier then or because I was immature, I can't say.

But regarding current Yank offerings, I've either lost part of my sense of humour or things have gone way down hill down south. I have sampled the most popular Yank humour on the tube and in the theatre. I will admit that, despite the availability of Yank humour, mine have been small samples, since I let exposure time be determined by how long-lasting were the effects of my Gravol or NoDoz—depending on what I was trying to appreciate.

But really, dear Yankee readers, my apologies, but get real: *South Park* is not funny or daring satire (unless you are in grade school in the Bible Belt), and most of your beloved Hollywood 'romantic comedies' are not at all comedic, and their only connection to romance is their tendency to send one to bed, alas only to sleep. Current so-called sit-coms are a lot more explicit than Mary Tyler Moore was, but actually far less funny. And if one tunes into the Comedy Network to sample the latest shticks of stand-up comics, one has little time to laugh, for one is too in awe of how incredibly crass the Yankee 'sensibility' has become.

Of course, as always, I'm over-generalizing—and all the *Seinfeld* and *Simpsons* fans are arming for a fight. Please drop your weapons! There undeniably are funny, even witty, American comics and American sitcoms and American movies. Most of my countrymen consume massive amounts of your humour—even those few with some taste. (And allegedly even sophisticated Parisians love Jerry Lewis slapstick.) You have Charlie Chaplin and Lenny Bruce and Woody Allen on your national CV: you can rest your case.

Nevertheless, my point is that although Yanks got lucky, big time, *sometimes*, the U.S. is a big country and overall—per capita—the quality of the humour, it seems to me, is roughly equivalent to the quality of the cuisine. Most of it is as tasteless as MacDonald's fries and as subtle as a Taco Bell taco. America has some fine restaurants and some brilliant and witty humorists, but the standard fare seems to be Big Macs with sloppy dressing and sloppily dressed comics with dirty mouths.

Now I've admitted that Canuck cuisine is an oxymoron, but we do have Canuck humour that I would say, albeit without sufficient linguistic skills or experience to back it up, is 'world class.' We're like the Brits, in this way, I'd say. We can't cook fer shit, but we can be very funny. Maybe we inherited part of it from our mother country—certainly a more fortunate inheritance than our appalling priggishness.

But to understand the origins of Canadian humour one has to look at all three of our primary cultural influences. Apropos this I came across this quotation from a Robert H. Winters: "You have perhaps heard the story of the four students - British, French, American, Canadian - who were asked to write an essay on elephants. The British student entitled his essay 'Elephants and the Empire'. The French student called his 'Love and the Elephant.' The title of the American student's essay was 'Bigger and Better Elephants.' And the Canadian student? He called his essay 'Elephants: A Federal or Provincial Responsibility?'

Okay, this is a mug's game, but let me attempt to delineate the major characteristics of British, French, American and Canadian humour as best I can—for the first three are clearly the influences that resulted in the last.

The Brits have a fondness for...
o   Dry and wry repartee or asides (ala Shakespeare)
o   Bathroom humour that requires one to be fixated at Freud's Anal Stage of Psychosocial Development
o   Humour that requires serious higher education to be appreciated (Cambridge or Oxford preferred)
o   Tits and ass humour that requires one to regress to the mental age of the early pubescent boy
o   Word play
o   Irony, yea even sarcasm.
o   Surrealism and the absurd
o   Class-based social situation humour
o   Well, actually just about any kind of humour, when you think about it

No matter what one's prejudices, it has to be admitted that the Brits are very, very funny. (I know, I know, sometimes it is unintentional.) From *Benny Hill* to *Monty Python*, from *Mr. Bean* to *Blackadder*, their humour spans the spectrum from ultraviolent to infrarediculous. Oh also, and at the far end of the electromagnetic spectrum, there is the out-there-in-far-outer-space *Red Dwarf*, a masterpiece of comedic sci-fi TV that rivals Douglas Adams' literary works.

The Frogs have a fondness for...
o   Farce and physical humour
o   Caricature and satire
o   Word play and the *mon bot* and sarcastic *riposte*
o   Sexual humour
o   Transsexual humour
o   Pansexual humour
o   Sex
o   Sex

It has been suggested that 'French humour' is an oxymoron. (I suspect it was the British who made the suggestion, but I can't document this.) It is true that the French Academy, that official guardian of the French Language, only accepted 'humoristique' as a legitimate French word in 1878—and then took until 1932 to approve the noun *humour*. But academician's attitudes aren't a good cultural benchmark. Remember that Dadaism originated on French soil! *Ubu Roi* reigns! And that fellow Voltaire, he was French wasn't he?

The Yanks have a fondness for:
o   Cutesy humour; e.g., so-called romantic comedies
o   Situational comedy
o   Crass humour
o   Racial and ethnic humour
o   Profanity
o   Righteous indignation
o   Black humour

I, personally, do not share these preferences, except for the last mentioned. But I know that personal taste, maybe even more than cultural considerations, determines what one finds funny—and that the diversity in personal taste is huge. Judgements as to what one finds humorous are gut reactions. And humour is special in that, unlike other aesthetic judgments, it is resistant to even quasi-objective evaluation. You may not initially have a positive emotional response to, say, a particular Beethoven symphony or a painting by Picasso or a poem by Dylan Thomas, but after being educated in the structure of the work, its historical significance, the allusions required to understand it, one can then return to the work and be profoundly moved. But, sorry, you'll never laugh at a joke that had to be explained!

I'm covering my ass here, admitting not only that my wild generalizations about the nature of different cultural preferences in humour are debatable, but also admitting that my taste may very well be totally idiosyncratic—and indefensible. Lord knows, my own family—for God's Sake!—is more likely to groan than laugh at my brilliant witticisms.

But I digress. The question is: What have Canucks taken from these three cultures to cobble together their own unique brand of humour. I would say we've taken the most from the Brits—for of course they have the most to offer. We seem especially adept at satire and parody, and while our humour is never as high-brow as high-brow British humour, it is more literate than most Yank humour. We dabble in all the other types, but I'd say that satire, parody, and caricature dominate.

But there is one special secret herb and spice to our humour. We stir into the borrowed cultural mix one ingredient that is used far more sparingly in Brit, Frog, or Yank humour: *self-deprecation*. We, unlike them, are not, nor have ever been, a world super-power, and so lack the self-importance that is so much ingrained in these three cultures. The British think everyone else in the world is uneducated compared to them. The French think they are the only people with refined aesthetic taste, be it in the fine arts or the culinary arts or the erotic arts. The Americans think anythin' that ain't American is inferior, over-priced, over-rated, and pretentious. (The French and the British may have a point.) Meanwhile, back at the farm, Canadians don't think they're superior to anyone except maybe the Yanks in terms of sophistication and common decency, and that meagre accomplishment isn't sufficient to give us dangerously elevated levels of self-esteem requiring medication.

.

So we make fun of ourselves a lot. Most Newfie jokes you'll hear will come from a Newfie. I recently watched the Winnipeg Comedy Festival and the theme was "Middle-age." Every single comedian was middle-aged and every comedian's shtick involved making (mostly) gentle fun of his or her own situation and frailties. Canadians seem to possess the admirable ability to mock and laugh at themselves.

.

Of course we also make fun of our neighbours, Albertans take swats at Torontonians, and jokes about Yanks aren't exactly a scarce commodity up here, but more often than not the joke is a two-edged sword. (I think we are not so much sarcastic as sardonic.) Consider this example. An American worried about Canada's allegedly strict laws about bringing weapons across the border writes a Canadian Travel Advisory Website asking: "Can I bring cutlery into Canada?" The answer: "Why bother? Just use your fingers like we do." Yeah, I don't find this gut-splittingly funny either, but it is typical of Canadian humour in that it mocks Yank ignorance while simultaneously making fun of ourselves.

.

Another example? A little more funny? Hmm. This book? (I hope.)

.

.

Update

Yank politics has become so absurd as to be considered comical in its own right. It has received so much press coverage up here that we 'get' and can appreciate a lot of American political satire. "The Daily Show" and "The Colbert Report" are extremely popular among my friends. I know these wits could be accused of shooting fish in a barrel. For example, one could argue that making fun of Fox News or those truly crazy Republicans isn't that difficult. But, think about it: it isn't easy to satirize what already seems like a satire. I will admit, however, there may be something a bit cruel about laughing at mentally challenged folks like Sarah Palin and Michelle Bachmann.

Alas, there isn't that much really good political satire of our own politicians, although Rick Mercer's rants are certainly worth noting.

Regional Diffs And Riffs

It is reasonable to think of Canada as having six major regions, roughly located and succinctly stereotyped below.

- The Far North
    - From west to east: *Yukon, Northwest Territories,* and *Nunavut* (formerly part of the Northwest Territories) hanging over all the other provinces like a giant glacier just waiting to slide down and crush all the little folk huddling in the warmth near the U.S. border.
    - Land of the midnight sun (in summer) and land of suicidal depression in the interminable dark of winter. They, along with the Scandinavians, invented the psychological disorder SAD ("Seasonal Affect Disorder")
    - Cold, sparsely populated by tough sons (and daughters) of bitches.
    - Cold.
    - Cold.
- The West Coast
    - *British Columbia* (Western most province, on the Pacific, if not politically pacific.)
    - A lala land ala California; sorta LA *with* good bud and *without* the bad attitude.
    - In the south the warmest, albeit wettest, climate in Canada.
    - Lush forests, grandiose mountains, and the roiling sea all a stone's throw from each other.
- The Prairies
    - From west to east: *Alberta, Saskatchewan, Manitoba*
    - Big sky; flat land.
    - In Saskatchewan and Manitoba, good place to watch grass grow—or, in Alberta, watch oil spurt from the ground and bank accounts grow.
    - Inhabited by cowboys and farmers, but range wars are a thing of the past.
- The Ontario
    - *Ontario*
    - The province that is the centre of the universe—at least according to its residents, but geographically east of Manitoba and roughly in the centre of Canada.

- Major city is Toronto: which is the *real* centre of the universe, for the rest of Ontario is just 'the provinces'—at least according to the Romans in Toronto.
  - Inhabitants vary from pseudo-sophisticates in "TO" to pseudo-rednecks in the North.
- La Belle Province
  - AKA *Quebec*
  - The province, wannabe sovereign state, that is the centre of the cultural universe—according to its residents, but geographically east of Ontario; i.e., to your right if you're looking at a map, albeit to the left if you're looking at a political diagram.
- The East Coast
  - Roughly from north to south the three 'new's: *Newfoundland* including Labrador, *New Brunswick*, and *Nova Scotia*—with little ol' *Prince Edward Island* easternmost off New Brunswick.
  - Poorest provinces with the wittiest and friendliest inhabitants.

The Far North

Yank Question: From everything you've said so far, I'm getting the impression that you're telling me that Eskimos and snowshoes and igloos and polar bears and Mounties with dog sleds are all a myth? That Canada is civilized?

Canuck Answer: No, I'm not implying that at all. Canada is *not* civilized, except perhaps in comparison to The States or Papua New Guinea. And we really do have that good romantic Real North, true and blue, stuff—or at least I and most Canadians think we do. But the fact is most of us just can't speak from personal experience. The True North is as much an urbanite's legend to us as it is to you.

So what to say about the Far North, the land that makes up *40%* of Canada's landmass and is home to less than *one-half of one percent* of Canada's population? I have virtually *nothing* to say. (Sighs of relief.)

I have nothing to say because I've never been there—like most Canadians. I have friends who have taught school in the high arctic. I've read news stories about wild goings-on in Yellowknife and Dawson City. I'm familiar with the doggerel of Robert Service. I've watched documentaries about polar bears and seal hunting. I've fantasized about visiting Wood Buffalo National Park on the edge of the Northwest Territories, Canada's largest wilderness park (44,807 square kilometres) and one of the largest in the world—and, of course, a major UNESCO Heritage Site.

But all I can say, and it *is* a guess, is, that for Yanks, Alaska (another place I've never been) is probably the closest analog to this part of my adopted country—although I strongly suspect most Canucks living in the far north would consider Alaska a cozy suburb in comparison to the Northern-most reaches of our arctic. And say that Anchorage is to Inuvik as Big Sur is to Furnace Creek in Death Valley. Or something like that.

Update

Since I, like most Canadians, really know virtually nothing about this huge part of our country, with its minuscule number of inhabitants, I certainly can't offer any update. I guess I could mention that the shabby way we treat the Inuit (translation for Yanks: "Eskimos") has finally made the news down here—at least more frequently than it has before.

BC: Big Coast Wannabes

Yank Question: Is it true your west coast is even wilder than our west coast?

Canuck Answer: Depends what you mean by 'wilder'. We have more badass bears and more big trees. Well, truth be told, maybe you Yanks might have even bigger trees on your west coast.

B.C.: Before Christ. It's a pagan place. B.C. is a wannabe California--with a vengeance. What is it that drives people to the edge, the edge of the continent? A vintage car, a wagon train, the lure of gold, a bad relationship, a fantasy about fame, a wannabe hip or hippie hopefulness? Dunno. I do know that the West Coast is the brink, and many folk at their personal brinks are driven to—or drive out to—the continental brink. I know I did when I took a break from a less than stellar first year at university and, with my roommate, drove the famous Route 66 from Chicago to L.A. (AKA, Lotus Land)—where we only managed to survive for a few months before tucking in our tails and heading back east.

Extremism is the name of the game all along North America's geologically shaky edge at the Pacific. I think the best way to understand B.C. is to think of it as very much like California: Pacific Ocean and Rocky Mountains, urbanity and wilderness, side by each. Yes, the Pacific is less pacific off the B.C. coast, and the Rockies are rockier than they are farther south. The urbanity is less urban or urbane, but the wilderness is wilder. The weather is slightly less temperate and it rains and snows more. The marijuana is better (I'm told) and the penalties for indulging are less. The politics are less fascistic, but perhaps even more bizarre than down south in California.

If you love L.A. or San Francisco, you'll love Vancouver. If you don't (as I don't), you won't. B.C. is probably the most American of the Canadian provinces—but only if matched up with California. (It bears no resemblance whatsoever to Alabama.)

There are actually at least four B.C.s. Vancouver is a country unto itself. Then there is The Interior and The Island. And finally there is the Far North of British Columbia—which bears more resemblance to the Northwest Territories or the Yukon than to the rest of the province.

Vancouver. If I see someone walking along the street with their shoulders hunched up, I always assume they've just moved from Vancouver where hunched shoulders to keep the rain from streaming down one's back is the standard posture. It is not quite as bad as Scotland where the average number of 'rain-free' days in the year can be counted on one hand, but it does rain, rain, rain a lot in Vancouver. The wet westerlies coming in from the Pacific Ocean hit the Rockies, and, unable to make the steep climb, jettison their H_2O on Vancouver. I performed a miracle by traveling to Vancouver nearly half a dozen times in a row without encountering rain, but the lushness of the vegetation was damn suspicious—and my next week-long visit included no dry days at all.

Their so-called 'winter' is the rainy season—or I should say the *rainiest* season. Now Canada doesn't have any place without real winter except southern B.C., so the lure of Vancouver is totally understandable, but there is a dear price to be paid for not having snow to shovel and below zero temperatures for half the year: that price is eternally grey skies that squeeze out intermittent but relentless, soul-eroding drizzle most days.

And of all Canadian cities, Vancouver is most like the typical Yank city in its having a distinct tenderloin district—the infamous East End. There at the intersection of Hastings and Main, or 'Wastings and Pain' as the locals call it, a visiting Yank can ease his homesickness even more effectively than by ducking into a MacDonald's. He'll find a reassuring and familiar cityscape filled with junkies and hookers and the hapless homeless—all virtually indistinguishable from those back home in Baltimore or New York. (Well, maybe they're more likely to politely thank you for a handout and less likely to mug you if you don't cough up.) The Hell's Angels even have a neat little club here.

That the losers and luckless end up in Vancouver is understandable because the climate, unpleasant as it may be, is less likely to kill someone without shelter than in wintry Winnipeg, Toronto or Edmonton. And that the crazies and the freaks end up in Vancouver follows from the North American tradition of routinely giving the command "Go West, young man, go West" to malcontents in the more conformist East. And the concern with the epidemic of hard-drugs means little attention is paid to those indulging in a little B.C. bud.

This is not to say that most of Vancouver isn't downright beautiful. Tucked in between the ocean on the west and the mountains on the east and a stone's throw (well—more accurately—a day's drive) from real, stark, and awe-inspiring wilderness, it rests in an ideal and idyllic location. Vancouver has an actual urban population of only half a million (two million if one counts the official metropolitan area), but it seems much larger, much more cosmopolitan than these numbers suggest.

Bottom line: a nice place to visit, but I, at least, wouldn't want to live there.

The Interior and The Island.
There are wonderfully diverse cultures and varied climates to be found in the other B.C. communities. The interior of B.C. has a major wine-growing area, the Okanagan Valley, which is one of the warmest regions in all of Canada. But the Northern interior has communities that rival the Northwest Territory for harshness of climate and frontier attitudes.

And then there is sparsely populated Vancouver Island, the largest North American island in the Pacific Ocean, with an area (12,408 sq. miles; 32,134 sq. km.) twice the area of all of the Hawaiian Islands together. It's an eco-Alice's Restaurant. What do you want? Rainforests, meadows, sand dunes, marshes, oceanic beaches, mountains, rivers, lakes? Vancouver Island has it all. Want to watch whales, fish for salmon, photograph exotic birds, uncover secret Gnostic hippie communes? Vancouver Island is for you. Into the arts? Visual artists, poets, and other eccentric misfits comprise a large portion of the small number of year round residents. One of my good friends, and a fine poet, lives in Campbell River. Another friend runs an arts-oriented resort at Gabriola Island. Salt Spring Island is a notorious refuge for artists. And there is even a city on the main island with a much nicer climate than mainland Vancouver's. Victoria, with a population of 335,000, is no longer very Victorian, except in its gardens, but it is a such a nice place to live that it is a popular retirement choice for Canucks fed up with shovelling snow. And it, like the rest of this furthest West area of Canada, is disproportionately concerned with the arts.

Sorry, I'm starting to sound like a tourist brochure—and starting to convince myself we should move out there. Hmm.

Update

Vancouver continues to grow, and its clothes no longer fit, because its hemmed in by the sea to west, the mountains to north and the east, and the U.S. border to the south. I was there again just over a year ago, and somehow the overcrowding hasn't decreased its attractiveness. But it has sent housing prices sky high (the only direction expansion is possible). That may have something to do with it at least seeming to be more populated by Yuppies than misfits and societal drop-outs. Residency on Vancouver Island, too, is still as attractive, but also becoming prohibitively expensive.

The Prairie Chickens

Yank Question: There really aren't cities called Moose Jaw and Saskatoon and Red Deer? And Medicine Hat! Someone is just pulling my leg, right?

Canuck Answer: Wrong. Yank legs are easy to pull, but these are real places. But if you can have cities named French Lick and Climax, I don't understand why you're surprised.

The Canadian Prairies could be compared to the American Midwest, but like comparing the Canadian Conservative Party to the Republican Party, the comparison has only the most superficial validity. The so-called Prairie Provinces (Alberta, Saskatchewan and Manitoba) are most defined by their geomorphology—not by their politics or any commonality of philosophy or cultural tradition.

I once took the train from Vancouver on the West Coast back to Ontario. It took three days, and each day a distinct landscape passed by my window. The first day was The Mountains. The second day was the Prairies. The last day was trees and rocks, rocks and trees, the Northern Boreal forest.

I haven't spent much time in the Prairie Provinces, so on this area of Canada I am even less qualified than usual to comment. I know the apparent homogeneity of the landscape as viewed from a train window is misleading: Alberta and Saskatchewan and Manitoba are very different places with very different political and social leanings. And the difference between, say, Northern Manitoba towns such as Churchhill (at the edge of the arctic) and Southern Manitoba cities such as Winnipeg (hugging the U.S. border) I am sure is also huge. So, to avoid embarrassing myself with more wild unfounded generalizations than I have so far been guilty of, I'll be quick and dirty.

Alberta.
Alberta is bounded on the west by the Rocky Mountains and including the famous, upscale ski resort town of Banff and its eastern boundary blurs into the great farm flatland that extends unbroken to the Ontario border. Its big Northern city is Edmonton, a modern and wealthy urban centre thriving in one of the harshest climates of any major city in the world. It's other, more southern city is Calgary, Canada's answer to the

American stereotype of The Wild West and home of the famous Calgary Stampede. Alberta is a rich province because of its oil resources. And being rich, it tends to be politically conservative. It would be insulting to compare it to Texas, for Albertans' necks are not nearly as red, but the two places do have something in common regarding attitudes, both admirable and distasteful. Alberta swaggers a bit. Alberta looks down on the pretensions of "Eastern Canada", by which they really mean Central Canada or, even more specifically, Torontonians with their superior airs. Alberta has more than a little of the Wild West mentality, including the prejudices and rough justice associated with that world view. (But unlike Texas, thank God, they don't carry it to the extend of endorsing capital punishment and murdering their own citizens. Nor do they throw the kid caught with a bit of weed into a snake pit prison for years.) Alberta oil fields pay big bucks to 'roughnecks' working the rigs, and it's rumoured that "safety first" isn't a motto on the sites, or "moderation in all things" the after-work policy. Albertans tend more toward *laissez-faire* capitalism, and aren't first in line to approve government regulation of their industry or entrepreneurs—even when such regulation is clearly justified for sound ecological reasons. Albertan politicians speak plainly and are quite willing to stand up to the federal government. In short, it seems a rather rough and ready kind of place, and it is probably the province that would most fit in with The United States, should it switch allegiances. (And talk of doing so does happen there.)

Saskatchewan.
This is the ultimate 'Prairie Province": Fields of wheat, barley, rape (oops, we have to be politically correct and use the word 'canola'), big sky, flatland as far as farsighted eye can see. It is an agricultural province, although it also has a substantial mining industry. Its two major cities are Saskatoon and Regina, the latter the more southern, but both not far from the border. Interestingly, like the U.S. prairie state of Iowa, which is a bit of a hotbed for literary activity and noted for the famous Iowa Writers' Workshop, so too is Saskatchewan the unlikely home for much serious literary and artistic activity. Its residents aren't all taciturn farmers, working the land, and spending their little free time on a rocker on the front porch. While in some ways I suppose it could be considered our "Middle Canada", just as Iowa and its neighbouring states are considered "Middle America", it differs drastically from its southern counterpart in terms of its politics. One might expect fiscal—typically 'farmerly'—conservativism to be the norm, but, surprise, surprise, Saskatchewan has a strong left-wing tradition and has more often than not embraced the most left-wing of major Canadian parties: the NDP. So, Toto, this isn't Kansas anymore—despite superficial appearances.

Manitoba.
I have spent the grand total of one half of an hour in Manitoba, so I cannot speak from any personal experience. The facts as I know them from research and hearsay follow. Winnipeg is the coldest, windiest major city in Canada—and some claim in the whole world! It also contains more than half the total population of the province—albeit that is only a bit more than half a million folks. It has a major artistic, literary and musical scene that is very happening. The Royal Winnipeg Ballet is highly respected internationally. The Winnipeg Art Gallery, the Manitoba Opera, the Manitoba Museum, and the Winnipeg Symphony Orchestra also enjoy an international reputation for excellence. If these folk are rednecks, they also are highbrows. And Manitoba tends, like its western neighbour to lean to the left politically. On the downside, it has the second highest crime rate for a Canadian city, only getting the silver, because Vancouver has the gold. (Still, it would seem like Pleasantville, Kansas to the average American urbanite, just as it would seem, culturally, like NYC to the average Middle American.)

Update

If my superficial generalizations about the Prairie Provinces need updating because of any major changes, I must have missed them. Certainly Alberta has been in the (bad) news a lot more lately, because of the destructive tar sands extraction of oil. I'm not alone in thinking it should be illegal, but it is strongly supported by our current Prime Minister who seems to think the term 'sustainability' refers to sustaining the incomes of Robber Barons.

Ontario: King Rats In A Dirty Nest

Yank Question: I always get confused. Is it Ontario, Toronto—or Toronto, Ontario?

Canuck Answer: It doesn't really matter. Toronto *is* Ontario. Well, at least that's what Torontonians think. (And I'll confess that when I first considered moving here, I was so ignorant as not to be sure which was right either!)

Southern Ontario, when a British territory (1774 to 1840), was known as "Upper Canada". ("Lower Canada" was in southern Quebec and consisted of part of the former French colony of New France.) The strong British influence on the mores and folkways (read: weird social behaviours) of Ontarians has slowly eroded away. (Unfortunately, what are replacing these are the mores and folkways of their southern neighbours.) I've already mentioned some of the confusions that I as an immigrant—a Yankee in The British Court—experienced upon arriving in Toronto. But probably the thing most relevant to any discussion of regional differences is the lingering superiority complex residents of this province feel—and especially its "Upper Canada" part—which surely is an inheritance from the Brits.

It's like those nested Russian dolls. My dad was important, so I'm important, albeit a bit less so, and my son is important, albeit even a little more less so. The sins of the father are delivered on to the son, and that includes the sin of *hubris*. The fact that Dad is no longer CEO takes a while to sink in. Hale Britannia. England was once the world's super power. The fact that now the British government seems to take orders from the White House has not yet filtered down to the general populace of The Empire, most of whom still feel superior to those rubes across The Pond.

Well Upper Canada, while so named simply because it was further up the St. Lawrence, always felt uppity, always felt superior to lowly Lower Canada, where those garlic eating Frenchies lived. The Upper Canadians may not have been Big Daddy England, but they were after all Daddy England's sons and daughters. The Imperial Order of Daughters of the Empire (I.O.D.E.) is still a major Canadian women's organization. It's a charitable organization—sort of a snooty version of the Shriners. (That's unfair: they both are major philanthropic organizations. The Shriners shouldn't be slandered—even if they wear funny hats. It might just be time to remind my readers not to send me indignant letters dusted with anthrax just because of my snide remarks: this book is all in fun. Well, mostly.)

So we have Southern Ontario, and especially Toronto, feeling excessive, unjustified self-esteem and the rest of Ontario feeling resentful of these wimps in the south having such a superior attitude—but, in turn, themselves feeling superior to the rest of Canada. Eggs inside of eggs. Ontario is the centre of the

Canadian Universe, and Toronto is the centre of the Ontario Universe. And those in Northern Ontario, those up on the map from Upper Canada, can take solace in the former assumption and take umbrage with the latter.

What about the rest of Canada? They think of Ontario as a self-important bully, much as Canadians tend to think of Americans. But just as the hard fact is that the U.S. has more power than Canada, so too does Ontario wield the most power of any of the Canadian provinces—in both cases because of population and wealth.

So to return to primer advice. Yanks can expect Ontario to be a mix of British and American flavours, and its residents to manifest the superiority complexes associated with both. Toronto, once nicknamed "Toronto The Good" because of its British repressive attitudes toward 'vice', be it sex or drink, is probably now more appropriately nicknamed "Toronto The Naughty" for its relatively easy going attitude toward such things—at least as compared to most of the Lower 48. Torontonians pride themselves on living in a 'world-class' city. And Toronto certainly is no hick-town, although clearly still a bit insecure about its status. (Paris doesn't have to advertise itself as a "world class city".) Toronto has great restaurants and great venues for art and entertainment, be it opera or rock 'n roll, ballet or jazz, baseball or poetry readings.

Since I first arrived there, it has become exponentially more cosmopolitan. Hell, it even has developed ghettos and gangs and managed a few drive-by shootings. If it really works at it, it could start to compete with the big bad cities in The States. (Maybe even get nicknamed Baltimore North?) But at the time of this writing, it still is one of the safest, cleanest big cities this side of The Pond. And while not quite the Alice's Restaurant that Montreal is, you can get *almost* anything you want there.

Northern Ontario, which for Upper Canada residents seems to begin at the outskirts of the Northern most suburbs of Toronto, is more difficult to describe. My home, North Bay, refers to itself as "The Gateway To The North" and is more than two hundred miles north of Toronto. And it yet is considered by anyone north of North Bay to still be Southern Ontario. Local residents resent this implication that we aren't as tough and hardy as those further up the latitude, but the fact is we are a border town. North of us most communities' economies are based on either logging or mining, while our town (of 55,000) has a diversified economic base of tourism, education, and industry.

Yanks who visit Northern Ontario can expect—more than in Toronto—a bit of the casual friendliness and frankness they are accustomed to back home. But what they shouldn't expect is all the amenities they'd find in their big cities—or Toronto. You can't get sushi in Moosenee or Kirkland Lake—or take in a production of *The Marriage of Figaro*. (You can, surprisingly, actually get sushi at one place in North Bay.) But of course tourists go to Northern Ontario to 'rough it' and surely can deal with only 12 stations on their motel TV. Go north for rocks and trees, trees and rocks, fish and game, lakes and rivers—and strip clubs and beer and being away from the missus.

Update

Toronto's ego has continued to grow, and unfortunately so has its less savoury similarities to big American cities. It now has what could fairly be called a neighbourhood slum with drug trade, gang warfare, shootings, and the whole toxic enchilada. (However, like Paris, it's on the outskirts, not in the city's core.) Still, the working class neighbourhood that is just a few blocks from the downtown, "Cabbagetown", has been gentrified, and the old 60's hip district, "Yorkville", is now embarrassingly upscale. But they were both well on the way to that transformation eight years ago.

Northern Ontario hasn't changed that much. Residents still resent Torontonians, and Torontonians still think cottage country is the real north—as, of course, so do Yank tourists.

Quebec: Big Pond Frogs

Yank Question: Is it safe to go to Quebec? I don't speak French. Will I be insulted?

Canuck Answer: Don't worry, for most Quebecers are friendly folk and they won't make fun of you. Baltimore is dangerous and full of rude folk—not Montreal. And no one in Quebec expects Yanks to be able to speak anything but Yank. My experience is that Yank tourists are more insulting and rude than any of their hosts—almost anywhere—so it is very strange for them to worry about being treated rudely.

Concern with the language 'issue' and imagined hostility toward Anglophones is probably the central concern of most Yank tourists and, less forgivably, also that of many Anglophone Canadians as well. While it is indisputable that many Francophone Quebecers have a bee in their bonnet about their language, it doesn't translate into hostility toward visitors to their province. Quebec may be a "distinct society", but it shares one trait with the rest of Canada: politeness.

The arrogance of the French is a cliché, and while having a grain of truth to it, it is often incorrectly confirmed because of a misunderstanding resulting from the reaction a foreigner gets when trying to use the native tongue. If you, an Anglophone, try to order a meal in, say, The Czech Republic or Lithuania, clumsily trying to speak their language, you will be greeted with astonishment and appreciation for your efforts. If you try to do so in France, or probably most other countries where the native language is a major one and most natives also speak English, you are more likely to have your server promptly switch to English, which he or she usually speaks more fluently than you do his or her language. The experience of a tourist speaking their language badly is for them a common one, and they're simply being knee-jerk polite and trying to make communication easiest for all involved. They do this so often they may appear cool, and the poor guy who is trying to show off his French to his girlfriend is likely to feel insulted—as if this damn waiter is laughing at his French and humiliating him in front of his lady. But this is certainly not the intent. What we have here is a failure to communicate—emotionally—because of a success at communication!

This misunderstanding is even more likely to occur in Quebec, and especially Montreal, than it is in Paris. To visit or live in Montreal, you don't *need* to speak a word of French—although knowing how to say please and thank you (*s'il vous plait* and *merci beaucoup*) would be nice, and, if living there, being able to recognize common, simple French expressions, especially questions, is useful. Most Montrealers are (far more than Parisians) fluently bilingual. Except in rural dominantly Francophone areas, Quebecers commonly mix the two languages in common discourse as they search for the best word or phrase for something. (This is considered by the very French French a debasement of the purity of their language, but that's another story.) So bilingual Quebecers easily detect an anglo-accent and so just naturally switch to English to make conversing easier. It is just the polite thing to do.

An aside, but a relevant anecdote. I remember many, many years ago going into a little shop in Holland, and trying to enquire about something. I'm a uni-lingual klutz, but I have a smattering of German, and I naively thought it might be more polite to try to speak German (their big neighbour's language and somewhat similar to Dutch) to the young girl behind the counter than to speak English—which I associated with American tourist arrogance. She promptly replied to me in French, for she obviously could tell my German was very minimal, and it seems she thought my accent indicated I was French. My French then was even more minimal than my German, so I, embarrassed, collapsed into English. She promptly responded in disturbingly proper English—with a distinct Oxford accent! This is a teenager working at a minimum wage job in a small shop, and yet she obviously spoke Dutch (her native tongue), German (well enough to tell I couldn't), French, and fluent English. What's that? Quad-lingual? I was humiliated and felt like a total ignoramus—but that certainly wasn't her intention.

Montreal is as much English as it is French, despite the best efforts of the extremist Language Nazis and the fascistic sign laws (Bill 101) which require all commercial establishments (be they in Chinatown or Anglo Westmount) to have their signs in French. And some of the townships outside the city are predominately English-speaking. But as one moves east into the heart of Quebec, one really will find fewer and fewer people, at least older people, who speak English. But this doesn't mean they are hostile to language-challenged visitors from The States or English Canada. On the contrary, they, like the Czechs and unlike the Montrealers, will respond with surprise and appreciation of any effort to communicate in their language. My son and daughter and I cycled from Montreal to Quebec City, and I remember the warm fuzzies I felt in every town and campground we passed through. One finds a sense of family and shared culture I've not found anywhere else in North America—except perhaps the Atlantic Provinces. I was amazed at the appreciation of our attempts to be polite visitors to their cultural enclave.

French Canadians feel besieged by monolithic English Canada, and when they take holidays, they rarely venture into what they view as the hostile territory outside their provincial borders. They go to other places in their province—or they go to France. My kids are bilingual, and so on this trip I had some small window looking into this Quebecois rural culture. We were considered oddities: Anglophones from what was perceived to be a hostile place, who inexplicably chose to holiday in their place. They seemed—flattered.

If I have one lasting impression from every visit to Quebec, it is one of warmth and friendliness and a very civilized European attitude toward life. How can you not like a people who love and value art and style and food and family and dogs and jazz and smoking and good times? (And whose women are so beautiful!) Oh, they may have a pickle up their butts about protecting their language and their culture, but it's a small pickle compared to anywhere else on this continent. (And besides it's probably a really good dill from one of the Jewish Delis in Montreal, maybe Ben's, or a crisp little *cornichon*.) Certainly their culture *is* worth preserving, and they can be forgiven for occasionally being a bit irrational and defensive about it.

So for the Yank who for whatever reason has not gone to Europe, Quebec is the closest approximation available on this continent.

Update

Whatever separatism was still significant in Quebec has diminished even more. However, Quebec still makes the news in Anglophone Canada with some of its Draconian provincial laws passed with the justification of protecting their version of French culture. Laws that annoy the more politically correct rest of the country, such as banning head scarfs in places of public employment, allegedly because it is a religious symbol. (Don't ask about the huge cross on the top of Mount Royal visible everywhere in the city or the nuns in their habits.) The requirements that new immigrants attend all French public schools also got a lot of Anglophones annoyed.

Meanwhile Montreal remains extremely tolerant and has become even more cosmopolitan—without apparently losing its distinct Quebecois identity.

Down East: Cod Fishers and Cod Pieces

Yank Question: What is your east coast like? Isn't that where they club those cute seal pups and breed our favourite breed of dog?

Canuck Answer: Better to club seals than to invade countries and club innocent civilians. Besides, seal meat is tasty; and while Labrador Retrievers may be a delicacy in Bejing, they're not on any Canadian menu. Also, Labs, of which I have two, are now bred primarily in the States, where, understandably, it is a seller's market for any warm-blooded creatures that are friendly, hardy, and loyal.

Ah, the East Coast! So you thought Moose Jaw and Medicine Hat were weird names for cities? Well tour the east coast and be sure to visit the thriving communities of Dildo and Come By Chance—and continue on to Conception Bay, finally winding up your seminal tour at Placentia! (What would Freud deduce about the inhabitants of this area based on their naming of towns?)

If Ontario and Quebec (Upper and Lower Canada) are the old boys, the establishment, then the Down East folk are the youngsters. And apparently proud of it, if the names of the provinces are any indication: *New* Brunswick, *Nova* Scotia, *New*foundland. The last mentioned only joined Canada, the Confederation, in 1949! (However the name "Newfoundland", or *Terra Nova*, given it by John Cabot in 1497, is allegedly the oldest European place name in North America. And, incidentally, should be pronounced "new-fun-land" with emphasis on the fun and de-emphasis on the land. Whether or not the middle syllable is apt is moot: the people are fun, the economy anything but.)

In talking about "Down East", as Canada's Atlantic Provinces are usually called, Newfoundland is the archetype. The Quebecois consider themselves a "distinct society", but Canadians residing on—or, like Newfoundland, *in*—the North Atlantic do so as well—and with just as much justification. And "Newfies" (the Canuck nickname supposedly given to them by Yanks after World War II, when U.S. military bases were set up there) are the most distinct of the distinct. Newfoundland's late entry into Canadian Confederation was not only belated, but reluctant as well, for in the plebiscite about joining Canada, the joiners won the majority by less than one percent.

The island of Newfoundland (fifteenth largest in the world) was 'discovered' by the Norse Vikings at least 500 years before Columbus sailed the ocean blue—although of course already inhabited by aboriginals (who could have done without being 'discovered' thank you very much) since 2500 B.C. (In 1960 the original and only authenticated Norse settlement in North America, L'Anse aux Meadows, was discovered at the northernmost tip of Newfoundland.) But Newfoundland's current distinct ethnic mix has little of the Norse. The French, British and the Irish influences are the primary ones; so much so that linguists talk of specific Newfoundland English, French and Irish dialects.

Newfies refer to their island as "The Rock", and the appellation is apt. It *is* a big, bloody, barren rock plopped in the North Atlantic Ocean off Canada's east coast. The communities are small and exist only along the coast. Fishing is the major 'industry', one which has been severely damaged by the depletion of the cod stocks which has increased the already severe poverty of the region.

You can't grow things on rocks, so Vegans should plan a Canadian holiday somewhere else—maybe in Vancouver, where food fetishists abound. My daughter bicycled up the coast to the northernmost tip of Newfoundland, and, while no vegetarian, she told me she came to crave a salad like a junkie craves a fix. Apparently, as in Eastern Europe and Russia, where city dwellers often have gardens out in the country, on The Rock the people living in the fishing communities drive up the one highway along their coast and plant private 'gardens' in the ditches beside the highway, where enough silt accumulates to grow some stunted root vegetables. Unfortunately, the moose (a far from endangered species here) tend to poach on the meagre harvest.

So when dining, whether at someone's home or at a restaurant, the visitor to this land shouldn't expect a thick steak, a baked potato, and a big chef's salad. One can however savour seal flipper pie, *brewis* (hard tack soaked in water, boiled and then cooked with that staple of the Newfie diet—salt cod and fat pork), finished off with a dessert of partridge-berry pie.

The Atlantic Provinces are Canada's poorest region, and Newfoundland is probably the poorest of the lot. The residents are not urbanites, and even the biggest cities are not big: St. John's, the capital of Newfoundland has a population of only 98,000, smaller than the aptly named Waco, Texas; and even Halifax, Nova Scotia (the largest city on the Canadian Eastern Seaboard) only has a population of 360,000. Yeah, that's roughly the same as that of cosmopolitan Wichita, Kansas. The Atlantic Provinces only account for a little over seven percent of Canada's population.

But what they lack in numbers, they make up in character. Let me speak of Newfies, keeping in mind that I'm following the Canuck tradition of calling anyone from Down East a 'Newfie'—matter not that they are from New Brunswick, Nova Scotia, or even potato land, Prince Edward Island. In much of Canada, Newfies are the butt of many jokes, viewed as hicks, Canuck hillbillies, especially in largely urbanized Ontario.

Question: "How do you confuse a Newfie?"
Answer: "You put his welfare check in a boot."

But the joke is on the jokers, for East Coast humour (by, not about) is in my opinion as major a contribution to the arts and civilization as Yankee jazz and blues or Italian pasta or French arrogant aesthetic pretentiousness. Well, maybe not quite.

Newfie Waiter: "Would you like to try the beef tongue?"
Mainlander: "No, I do not eat anything that comes from an animal's mouth."
Newfie Waiter: "Would you like an omelette instead?"

For my money, Newfies are among the wittiest people on the planet. Those folk on The Rock—well, hell, they rock! And even while they stand distinct from the rest of the country, they epitomize the humour of Canada—self-deprecating, sardonic, acerbic and wry. A humour that is as tough on the source as on the target. When my wife and I first moved to Toronto, the tenants in the flat above ours were from New Brunswick and they'd occasionally join us for a few brews. When the fella started telling stories, you'd have to put your mug down for fear you'd break up and sputter and choke as he dropped one after another surprise witticism in the course of his narrative, always delivered with a straight face and the distinct Newfie accent.

They're eccentric and non-conformist, dem folk down east. Of that there is no question. The Newfies can't even conform to time-zone conventions, which for some reason they choose to meet the rest of the world only half-way. When the CBC announces programming times it goes like: "at 3:00 p.m. Pacific, 4:00 p.m. Mountain; 5:00 p.m. Central,

6:00 p.m. Eastern, 7:00 p.m. Atlantic, and *7:30* p.m. Newfoundland." Go figure.

The other major Down East characteristic is that they're friendly—very friendly. Friendly to the point of embarrassing the far more reserved Canadians from west of them. Friendly to the point of probably making even putatively outgoing and friendly Yanks paranoid: "Nobody can be that nice without an ulterior motive." When I was in Halifax for a conference, the chief conversational competition at days end was seeing who could report the most outrageous act of friendliness they'd encountered that day. Here is but one example. A colleague went into a restaurant for breakfast. All the booths and tables were taken and the waitress apologized profusely and then rushed over to a booth where two cops were noshing eggs and bacon. One of the cops jumped up and hurried over to my friend and insisted he join them. Then after breakfast, coffee, a few smokes, and conversation (no, not interrogation), the cops insisted on driving him back to the hotel: four blocks was too far for him to walk on such a windy autumn day, and, besides, they had no calls! Before they left they tipped the waitress generously, refusing any contribution from my colleague. Jesu! This sort of story is enough to make one believe that dubious claim that "The Police are your friends!"

.

.

.

Update

.

Can't say much by way of an update, for as far as I can tell, the Maritimes are still the Maritimes in all their charm. My wife and I are heading 'down east' in a few weeks, and I don't expect anything to have changed so much as to require any revisions to this section.

Final Words—Of Apology

I said in my introduction, and in my defence, that what I had to say I felt I had a right to say, a *familial* right, because, in terms of nations, my parents are America and Canada; and kids have a right to say rude things about their parents, a privilege denied those outside the family. I'm sure that now having said these rude things, I am now disowned by both of those who raised and shaped me—which is also a right, a right that parents have. It would be hypocritical of me to say "no offence intended", for in many cases offence *was* intended. But I do want to say a few final, less acerbic, less sarcastic, words about my fatherland and adopted motherland. It's the Canuck in me: I have a deep need to apologize after I slip up and speak my mind.

I am—to a disturbing extent—what I am, because of both of my parent's influences. And being more or less self-satisfied with what I am (at least on alternate Tuesdays), I feel I should thank both lands for what they have given me.

The United States of America gave me a profound belief in the greater importance of the individual over any collectivity. My conviction of the importance of religious freedom, which has as a necessary corollary the separation of church and state, is certainly another inheritance from my Fatherland. America also contributed to my—admittedly and unabashedly absolutist—moral system which ranks human rights as unquestionably *the* most important ethical consideration. It also had much to do with my embracing the three primary tenets of Amnesty International: thou shalt not kill; thou shalt not torture; thou shalt not imprison a person for expression of their beliefs—no matter how offensive they may be to so-called 'community standards' or the powers that be. Sadly, these three principles seem to have been forgotten by too many Americans today.

As I think about it, I suppose the fact that *all* these convictions were engendered in me partially because of my American heritage is very paradoxical—given the reality of life in the so-called "Land Of The Free And Home Of The Brave". A country that right now is so flagrantly killing, torturing and unjustly imprisoning its citizens (and even citizens of other sovereign nations) isn't exactly what most people would call a 'role model'. Separation of Church and State? Gimme a break! God (as defined by Middle America) has reared his ugly, hoary head, just when we thought most optimistically that he was dead. And anyone with two neurons to rub together knows the American Dream is a pipe dream bearing no relationship to the much more real American Nightmare that only too many Americans are living.

But I'm not sounding grateful, and *I really am grateful*. I'm grateful to Jefferson and the creators of the Constitution and the Bill of Rights and all those who subsequently toiled in the field they planted—the civil rights activists and the American Civil Liberties Union and the many who within the educational system or on the mean streets continue to promulgate these values. I'm grateful for having, while growing up there, inculcated in me the values that The United States of America has at its original philosophical core: individualism, civil and human rights, freedom of expression, balance of power between the legislative, executive and judicial branches of government, separation of church and state, free enterprise, respect for initiative and innovation, tolerance for diversity, willingness to welcome immigrants and refugees, and, above all, a profound sense of the inviolable dignity and inalienable human rights of every man, woman and child.

I'm also grateful for the profound cultural and intellectual contributions Americans have made to civilization, as everyone should be. America, perhaps more than other nation has valued individualism, and in turn American *individuals* have contributed so very, very much! I can only hope that this individualism can weather the collectivistic, fervent nationalistic storm that seems to signal a horrible climate change below the border.

And Canada? Well, I will always be infinitely grateful to my adoptive motherland which gave me sanctuary when I most needed it. It is only too common for people to say "I love my country." I don't want to say that. I love my wife. Loving a whole country requires a far bigger heart than I possess. Better get Jesus on the cell phone for that kind of universal loving.

But I do feel toward the land in which I now reside a very deep affection. I really like the landscape, the ubiquitous rocks and trees and rocks and trees and rocks and trees. I like the self-deprecating humour indigenous to the area. I like the (until recently) usually relatively harmless absurdity of our politics. I like—have come to like—vinegar on my fries. I like knowing there is a so-called "social safety net" and that those that get ill can get proper medical care no matter their financial situation. I like most of my fellow citizens, who while often are a little too complacent for my taste, are so fundamentally *decent*. Sure, my adopted home has certain attributes that drive me crazy. The many snide remarks I've made about my adopted Motherland should make it obvious what it is about her that drives me to drink. (Not that I needed a ride.)

But I must say that I *really* like living here. I wouldn't want to live anywhere else (even though I much appreciate regular respites in Europe, where *their* quirks seem mere quirks, rather than daily, relentless annoyances.). And I am pleased my children had the opportunity to grow up here and have been able to reap the many benefits that are not available in my Fatherland.

So let me close this admittedly annoying book with a quotation from an old TV show that says it all: *"Hey, I only make fun of you cuz I love ya both—despite your foibles!"*

Oh, one other closing remark seems appropriate. As the curmudgeon composer Johannes Brahms allegedly said upon departing from a party where he'd been particularly obstreperous: "If there is anyone I neglected to insult, I sincerely *apologize*!" (He would've made a good Canuck.)

AUTHOR'S NOTE

"I believe that literature, like science, is a way of exploring different perspectives; and I believe that the results of these literary explorations, like the results of science, are always inherently tentative. It is for this reason that I choose to call my major works *hypotheses*. *Explaining Canada: A Primer For Yanks*, originally completed on 6 June 2006, is *Hypothesis 13*."

ABOUT THE AUTHOR

Ken Stange is the author of 14 books of poetry and fiction, hundreds of publications in literary and scientific journals, and winner of the 2011 Exile/Vanderbilt prize for short fiction. He is also a visual artist and Professor Emeritus at Nipissing University where he continues to teach "The Psychology of Art" as an online course. His special interest is the relationship of art and science and creativity. He remains glad to have become a Canuck.